The People of
THE NORTHERN HIGHLANDS
1600-1699

By
David Dobson

Copyright © 2023
by David Dobson
All Rights Reserved

Published for Clearfield Company by
Genealogical Publishing Company
Baltimore, Maryland
2023

ISBN: 9780806359663

Introduction

This book identifies many of the people of the counties of Caithness, Sutherland, and Inverness-shire during the seventeenth century. The region mostly lies west and north of the Great Glen apart from a portion of Inverness-shire which lies east of Lochs Lochy, Oich, and Ness.

The population was relatively sparse with only a few small burghs mostly lying along the east coast, all of which had medieval origins. The burghs were Dingwall, Tain, Fortrose, Cromarty, Dornoch, Wick, and Inverness, with Scrabster and Thurso by the Pentland Firth, and Kingussie lying within the highlands. The only sizable burgh was Inverness. The people at the time were overwhelmingly Gaelic speakers, with Lowland Scots -- who spoke a dialect of English -- settled in the burghs. Similarly, place-names were predominantly in Gaelic though a few were based on Norse originals, such as Ullapool, based on Ulapul -- Norse for 'Wolf farm'-- or Wick, from Vik the Norse for 'bay'. Several local surnames superficially in Gaelic include a Norse element, such as McLeod or MacLeoid from the Norse 'son of Ljotr', or MacCorquodale based on the Norwegian personal name 'Thorketill'. There are also a few placenames indicating a Pictish origin, dating before 1000 AD, such as Petty, or Pitcalnie, or Pitkerrie. The Picts inhabited much of Scotland before the early Middle Ages, while the Norse Vikings settled in the Northern Isles, the Hebrides, and what is now Caithness and Sutherland [Suderland in Norse]. In the Medieval period the inhabitants spoke Norn, a Norse dialect, in such localities. However, by the seventeenth century Gaelic and Scots English were predominant. The Reformation of the sixteenth century resulted in Scotland becoming officially a Protestant nation; however, in parts of the Highlands there were Roman Catholic enclaves, notably in Inverness-shire and on Barra.

Migration outwards from the Northern Highlands was initially small scale, apart from mercenaries who were recruited to fight for Scandinavia and the Netherlands, many of whom settled there. The Wars of the Three Kingdoms, 1638-1651, led to enforced emigration or the transportation of prisoners of war, most of whom were captured at the Battle of Dunbar in 1650 or the Siege of Worcester in 1651. These men were banished to the English colonies in the Caribbean, notably Barbados, or to Virginia and New England; they can be identified by their distinctive local surnames. Large-scale emigration from the Northern Highlands began in the eighteenth century and especially after the Highland Clearances of the mid-nineteenth century. The main clans or families during the seventeenth century were Sinclairs, Mackays, Sutherlands, McLeods, Rosses, Stewarts, McKenzies, Munros, Urquharts, Frasers, McDonnells, Chisholms, MacPhersons, McGillivrays, Davidsons, McKinnons, MacDonalds, McLeans, Camerons, Gunns, and Roses.

David Dobson, Dundee, Scotland, 2023

REFERENCES

ABR Aberdeen Burgess Roll

APS Acts of the Parliaments of Scotland

ASW Aberdeen Shore Works

BK Battle of Killiecrankie

BM Book of Mackay

CAG Compedium of American Genealogy

Cal.SPCol. Calendar of State Papers, Colonial

CF Chronicle of the Frasers

CRD Church Records in Danzig

CTC Scotland and the Commonwealth

EMA Emigrant Ministers to America, 1690-1811

ETR Edinburgh Tolbooth Records, 1657-1686

EVI Early Virginia Immigrants, 1623-1666

F Fasti Ecclesiae Scoticanae

FPA Fulham Papers, American

GAR Rotterdam Archives

H2 Omitted Chapters from Hotten's

ICB Inverness Court Book [SC]

IMB Inverness Town Council, Minute Book, [SC]

IR Innes Review, series

JMHSB Journal Museum & Historical Society Barbados, series

KEITH A Historical Catalogue of the Scottish Bishops

LLNV Lost Lives New Voices

MCM Maitland Club Miscellany

MGIF Military Governors of Imperial Frontiers

NCSA North Carolina State Archives

NEHGS New England Historic Genealogical Society

NJSA New Jersey State Archives

NRS National Records of Scotland

NWI New World Immigrants

NYHist.MS.Dutch New York Historical Manuscripts, Dutch

OPS Origines parochiales Scotiae

P Prisoners of the '45

PID Presbyterie of Inverness and Dingwall, 1643-1688

RAK Copenhagen Archives, Denmark

REA Register of Edinburgh Apprentices

REB Rollf of Edinburgh Burgesses

RSC Records of the Scots Colleges

RGS Register of the Great Seal of Scotland, series

RPCS Register of the Privy Council of Scotland, series

SAA Should Auld Acquaintance Be Forgot…1450-1707

SC Spalding Club

SCHR Scottish Church History Records, series

SCP The Scots College in Paris, 1603-1792

SCS Scots Charitable Society of Boston

SF Scots in Franconia

SG Scottish Genealogist

SHS Scottish History Society

SIG Scots in Germany

SIS Scots in Sweden

SP The Scottish Peerage

SPAWI State Papers, America and the West Indies

SRS Scottish Records Society

TGSI Transactions of the Gaelic Society of Inverness

WBA West Brabant Archives

ZA Zeere Archives

GLOSSARY

Baillie = a burgh magistrate

Barony = land held by a baron

Baxter = baker

Brother-german = a full-blooded brother

Brouster = a brewer

Caird = a craftsman

Carse = meadow land by a river

Chamberlain = a steward or factor

Chapman = a hawker

Comm. = Commissary court, used for confirming testaments, pre 1823

Cordiner = shoemaker

Dean of Guild = head of the merchant guild of a burgh

Ferrier = a blacksmith who shoes horses

Feu = a duty due to a superior

Feuar/fiar = a person who holds land in feu

Freeman = one with full membership of a guild or trade

Guilds-brother = a member of the merchant guild

Hearth-tax = a tax on every fireplace

Litster = a dyer

Maltman = a maltster

Mort cloth = a cover over a coffin on way to the grave

Poinding = to seize a debtor's goods

Provost = head of a Scottish burgh

Relict = a widow

Regality = similar to a barony but under an officer appointed by the king, so not heritable

Sasine = a document re transfer of property

Stent = a levy or tax on property

Tack = a lease

Tacksman= one who leased land directly from the landowner then sublet it to lesser tenants

Wadset = a contract

Webster/Wobster = a weaver

Wentner = a chimney sweep

Writer = a lawyer

Funeral in Glen Outil, Skye

Farming life in 1690

Huts in Uig, Lewis, Inhabitted 1859

Funeral in Glen Outil, Skye

Farming life in 1690

Huts in Uig, Lewis, Inhabitted 1859

John O'Groats, village northeast of Canisbay, Caithness, in the far north of Scotland

Loch Maree, with Ben Slioch

Sir Rorie Mackenzie of Tarbat

Tarbat House, c. 1700, built for George Mackenzie, 1st Earl of Cromartie, in Kilmuir-Easter Parish, Ross and Cromarty, near Nigg Bay

PEOPLE OF THE NORTHERN HIGHLANDS, 1600-1699.

ABERCROMBIE, JOHN, the burgh advocate of Inverness, [Inbhir Nis], by 1643. [IMB.202]

ABERNETHY, JOHN, the Bishop of Caithness, [Galllaibh], a letter to Sir Robert Kerr of Ancrum, dated 16 October 1623. [NRS.GD40.2.13.32]

ABERNETHIE, WILLIAM, late minister at St Peter's in Thurso, [Inbhir Theorsa], Caithness, sasines [NRS.RS36.111, etc]; testament in 1662, Comm. Caithness. [NRS]

ABRAHAM, GEORGE, a councillor of Inverness in 1642/1644. [IMB.181/182]

ABRAHAM, MARGARET, in Inverness, a testament, 20 November 1630, Comm. Inverness. [NRS]

ADAMSON, WILLIAM, a merchant in Thurso, Caithness, testament, 16 July 1662, Comm. Caithness. [NRS]

ALISTER [ALEXANDER] VIC CONCHIE, MARIE, an alleged witch in Inverness, [Inbhir Nis], in 1662. [TGSI.IX.119]

ALLAN, MAGNUS, in Lochside of Olrik, Caithness, testament, 10 December 1662, Comm. Caithness. [NRS]

ANDERSON, ALEXANDER FRASER MCSIM, in Inches, [Inshes], Inverness-shire, was subjected to a precept of poinding for payment of a bond due to James MacIntosh a merchant in Inverness, on 31 July 1690. [NRS.GD23.10.302]

ANDERSON, ANDREW, graduated MA from St Andrews University, in 1621, minister at Kildonan, Sutherland, from 1656 until 1664. [F.7.90]

ANDERSON, GEORGE, a periwig-maker, was appointed as Lieutenan of a Militia Company, to protect Inverness from McDonald of Keppoch, [A'Cheapach], and his rebels, 3 September 1688. [IMB.7]

ANDERSON, GILBERT, of Udol, [Uadal], Cromarty, [Cromba], graduated MA from King's College, Aberdeen, in 1626, minister at Cromarty from 1642 until his death in November 1655. [F.VII.4]

ANDERSON, HUGH, of Udol, Cromarty, son of the above Gilbert Anderson, graduated MA from King's College, Aberdeen, in 1651, minister at Cromarty from 1656 until deprived in 1673, returned in 1690, he died on 3 June 1704. [F.VII.4]; husband of Grisel Rue, a sasine around 1683. [NRS.RS38.V.438]

ANDERSON, HUGH, from Cromarty, a student at King's College, Aberdeen, in 1674. [KCA]

ANDERSON, ISABEL, spouse of Thomas Taylor a maltman in Inverness, a testament, 15 September 1631, Comm. Inverness. [NRS]

ANDERSON, JAMES, from Ross-shire, a student at King's College, Aberdeen, in 1663. [KCA]

ANDERSON, JOHN, a seaman in Inverness, a deed in 1706. [NRS.RD4.98.21]

ANDERSON, KENNETH, versus Rorie Fuller re an unpaid bond, in 1677, also Andrew Monro, a merchant in Dingwall, [Inbhir Pheofharain], Easter Ross, also concerning an unpaid bond. [NRS.GD71.81]

ANDERSON, WALTER, minister at Farr, Sutherland, from 1585 until 1603. [F.VII.106]; minister at Kildonan, Sutherland, from 1602 until 1615. [F.7.90]

ANDERSON, WILLIAM, burgh officer of Inverness was deposed on 3 October 1670. [IMB.243]

ANGUS, HUTCHEON, master of the William of Inverness, also the John of Inverness, and the Katherine of Inverness, trading with Aberdeen in 1665. [ASW.514/521/523]

ANGUS, JAMES, master of the William of Inverness arrived in Inverness from Le Havre in France on 10 March 1669. [NRS.E72.11.2]

ANGUSSON, WILLIAM, in Harpisdaill, Caithness, testament, July 1663, Comm. Caithness. [NRS]

ANNAND, Mr JOHN, a minister in Inverness, a reference on 31 March 1641. [IMB.178]

AWAIRSE, JOHN, in Gillies, Caithness, was to be apprehended as a rebel in 1670. [RPCS.III.194]

BAILLIE, ALEXANDER, of Dunyean, with David, William, John, and Robert his brethren, rebels around 1638, appeared, armed with swords, targes, guns, pistols, and other arms, at the burial of Christian Paterson, spouse of John Gordon, on 10 August 1642 where William Baillie stabbed Alexander Cuthbert Jamieson. [IMB.181]

BAILLIE, ALEXANDER, a burgess of Inverness, testament, 16 December 1668, Comm. Inverness. [NRS]

BAILLIE, ALEXANDER, born 1668, son of Alexander Baillie of Shirell, was a student at the Scots College at Douai, Flanders, in 1682. [RSC.1.56]

BAILLIE, ALEXANDER, of Torbreack, testament, 3 September 1679, Comm. Inverness. [NRS]

BAILLIE, DAVID, a Quartermaster of Fraser's Dragoons in 1646 during the Wars of the Three Kingdoms.

BAILLIE, DAVID, in Kinmyles, [Ceann a' Mhilidh], Inverness-shire, only son of the late William Baillie sometime Treasurer of Inverness, was admitted as a burgess and guilds-brother of Inverness on 20 September 1686. [IMB.344]

BAILLIE, DAVID, a brewer in Castle Street, Inverness, was admitted as a burgess and guilds-brother there on 8 November 1686. [IMB.7]

BAILLIE, FRANCIS, in Kinmylie, testament, 23 September 1676. [NRS]

BAILLIE, HARRY, from Inverness, a student at King's College, Aberdeen, in 1663. [KCA]; applied to become schoolmaster of Inverness, without success, on 20 September 1669. [IMB.237]

BAILLIE, HUGH, the younger, a writer [lawyer] in Fortrose, [A'Chananaich], Easter Ross, and his wife Isobel Hood, purchased land in Arcan, Urray, [Urrach], Ross-shire, from James MacLean, a bailie of Inverness, on 18 July 1692. [NRS.GD46.6.70]

BAILLIE, ISABEL, spouse of James Fraser in Dundelchak, testament 24 December 1680, Comm. Inverness. [NRS]

BAILLIE, JAMES, a member of Fraser's Dragoons in 1645 during the Wars of the Three Kingdoms.

BAILLIE, MARY, spouse of William McIntosh of Borlum, Inverness-shire, a bond dated 10 July 1661. [NRS.RD3.1.428]

BAILLIE, ROBERT, [1672-1726], minister of Inverness, papers 1704-1705. [NRS.NRAS.1091]

BAILLIE, WILLIAM, the younger, in Inverness in 1643. [IMB.193]; was appointed assistant shore-master on 15 October 1649. [IMB.203]

BAILLIE, WILLIAM, the younger, was described as an ill-affected and malicious neighbour of Inverness on 19 March 1666. [IMB.228]

BAILLIE, WILLIAM, the elder, a stent [tax] collector in Inverness on 19 April 1672. [IMB.252]

BAILLIE, WILLIAM, a burgess of Inverness, testament, 15 March 1676, Comm. Inverness. [NRS]

BAILLIE, WILLIAM, the Commissary Depute of Inverness on 3 January 1679, co-owner of the Dolphin. [NRS.AC7.5]

BAILLIE, WILLIAM, was admitted to the Scots Charitable Society of Boston, Massachusetts in 1698. [NEHGS/SCS]

BALMANNO, ADAM, in Thurso, Caithness, testament, July 1663, Comm. Caithness. [NRS]

BANNERMAN, Sir ALEXANDER, of Elsick, was admitted as a burgess of Inverness on 6 January 1709. [NRS.NRAS.64.3]

BARBOUR, ALEXANDER, a councillor of Inverness on 20 April 1644. [IMB.182]; was appointed stent [tax] collector for the Domsdaill of Inverness on 14 December 1644. [IMB.186]; treasurer of Inverness on 17 July 1654. [IMB.209]

BARBER, GEORGE, deceased, late resident near Rosemarkie, [Ros Mhaircnidh], Easter Ross, in 1654. [RGSS.X.356]

BARBOUR, JOHN, was appointed as Captain of a Militia Company, to protect Inverness from McDonald of Keppoch and his rebels, on 3 September 1688. [IMB.7]

BARBOUR, ROBERT, was granted the right to operate a ferry across the River Ness on 14 October 1664. [IMB.221]; applied to build a waulk-miln, [a fulling-mill], on the old dock, a waulker's, [fuller's], house, and a dam to supply water for the mill, on 9 January 1671. [IMB.245]

BARBOUR, ROBERT, of Mulderg, was appointed as a bailie of Inverness for 1676-1677 on 26 September 1676, [IMB.270]; as Dean of Guild, took the Test Oath on 19 December 1681. [IMB.299] ; was appointed as Commissioner for Inverness at the forthcoming Convention of Royal Burghs in Edinburgh on 5 July 1688. [IMB.7]

BARNES, ROBERT, Dean of Guild of Inverness, on 28 September 1670, [IMB.238]; also, on 9 April 1679. [NRS.AC7.5]

BARNMAN, DONALD, in Diren, Caithness, a testament, 11 April 1662, Comm. Caithness. [NRS]

BAYNE, [BAN], ALEXANDER, of Knockbaine, [An Cnoc Ban], Dingwall, Easter Ross, admitted participating in the Royalist uprising led by Mackenzie of Pluscarden and Lord Reay at the Battle of Balvenie in 1649. [SHS.24.157] [NRS.CH2.92.1]

BAYNE, ALEXANDER, of Tarradaill, in Urray or Kilchrist, participated in the rebellion under James Graham, Marquis of Montrose, in 1649. [SHS.24.159]

BAYNE, ANGUS, in Dornoch, Sutherland, paid his Hearth Tax in 1694. [NRS.E69.23.1.3]

BAYNE, Captain, of Brahan, [Brathann],in Urray or Kilchrist, Ross-shire, participated in the rebellion under James Graham, Marquis of Montrose, at Inverness and the Battle of Balvenie, in 1649. [SHS.24.159/162]

BAYNE, ALEXANDER, a property owner in Dingwall, a reference in 1652. [RGSS.X.16]; a bailie and merchant in Dingwall, Ross-shire, and his wife Katherine, re a bond with Sir Alexander McKenzie of Coul, [A'Chuil], in 1660s. [NRS.GD1.1149.17]

BAYNE, FARQUHAR, in Bellasder, Duthall, testament, 29 February 1632, Comm. Inverness. [NRS]

BAYNE, JOHN, in Daviot, [Deimhidh], Inverness-shire, testament, 15 August 1678, Comm. Inverness. [NRS]

BAYNE, JOHN, from Dingwall, admitted participating in the Royalist uprising led by James Graham, the Marquis of Montrose, into England and in the north of Scotland in 1649. [SHS.24.158] [NRS.CH2.92.1]

BAYNE, JOHN, a property owner in Dingwall, Easter Ross, a reference in 1652.
[RGSS.X.16]

BAYNE, KENNETH, a property owner in Dingwall, Easter Ross, a reference in 1652. [RGSS.X.16]

BAYNE, MARGARET, spouse of Finlay Gordon a cordiner in Inverness, testament, 2 October 1630. [NRS]

BAYNE, RONALD, from Ross-shire, a student at King's College, Aberdeen, in 1660. [KCA]

BAYNE, RONALD, of Knockbayne, [An Cnoc Ban], Ross-shire bailie of Dingwall, a Commissioner to the Convention of Royal Burghs on 14 July 1676. [IMB.268]

BAYNE, WILLIAM, in Okingill, Caithness, testament, 20 October 1662, Comm. Caithness. [NRS]

BEATON, MALCOLM, a Catholic in Kanloid, Arisaig, Inverness-shire, around 1701.

BELL, THOMAS, in Dornoch, Sutherland, paid his Hearth Tax in 1694. [NRS.E69.23.1.3]

BISHOP, FRANCIS, in Inverness in 1643. [IMB.193]; dead by 20 March 1665. [IMB.222]

BISHOP, FRANCIS, a glover in Inverness, second son of John Bishop a carpenter there, was admitted as a burgess and freeman of Inverness on 11 October 1686. [IMB.7]

BOSWELL, ROBERT, master of the Isobel of Inverness and later of the William of Inverness trading between London and Inverness in 1669. [NRS.E72.11.2]

BOWAR, WILLAM, in Mid Clyth, Caithness, a testament 1 July 1661, Comm. Caithness. [NRS]

BOWYER, FRANCIS, born in 1683, a schoolmaster at Morar, Inverness-shire, a Jacobite who was transported to the West Indies on 20 March 1747. [P.2.44]

BOYNE WILLIAM, from Caithness, a student at King's College, Aberdeen, in 1663. [KCA]

BROBNER, DONALD, in Freswick, Caithness, testament, 1662, Comm. Caithness. [NRS]

BRODIE, JACK, a soldier, married Jannegie Cornelis from Utrecht, in the Netherlands, there on 27 September 1612. [Utrecht Marriage Register]

BRUCE, DAVID, from Caithness, a student at King's College, Aberdeen in 1668. [KCA]

BRUCE, Mr ROBERT, in Caithness, a letter to Lord Ross, dated 5 August 1633. [NRS.GD3.13.4]

BRUCE, WALTER, from Caithness, a student at King's College, Aberdeen, in 1670. [KCA]

BRUIN, ALEXANDER, from Sutherland, a student at King's College, Aberdeen, in 1667. [KCA]

BUCHANAN, JOHN, of Ross, and his wife Margaret Stirling, a bond with William Buchanan in the West Mains of Buchanan, on 1 January 1692. [NRS.GD47.899]

BUYE, DONALD, a shipmaster in Inverness in 1681. [RPCS.XI.530]

BUY, or MCKENZIE, WILLIAM, in Inverness on 25 October 1667. [IMB.233]

BUYNACH, DUNCAN, in Inverness on 25 October 1667. [IMB.233]

CADELL, ROBERT, a merchant burgess of Wick, [Inhir Uige], Caithness, a sasine dated 23 January 1686. [NRS.NRAS.3094.466]

CAIRD, KENNETH, in Urray, [Urrath], or Kilchrist, participated in the rebellion under James Graham, Marquis of Montrose, in 1649. [SHS.24.159]

CALDER, ALEXANDER, from Caithness, a student at King's College, Aberdeen, in 1667. [KCA]

CALDER, JANET, spouse of William Tulloch a maltman burgess of Inverness, testament, 24 June 1634, Comm. Inverness. [NRS]

CALDER, WILLIAM, from Caithness, a student at King's College, Aberdeen, in 1668. [KCA]

CAMERON, or BODACH, EWAN, in Urquhart, testament, 15 April 1667, Comm. Inverness. [NRS]

CAMPBELL, ALEXANDER, a merchant in Stornaway, [Stornabhagh], Lewis, in 1706. [TGSI.XLIV.315]

CAMPBELL, alias MCGREGOR, DUNCAN, in the Mill of Tain, Ross-shire, in 1700. [NRS.AC9.229]

CAMPBELL, EVANDER, from the Isle of Lewis, [Leodhas], a student at King's College, Aberdeen, in 1667. [KCA]

CAMPBELL, JOHN, of Castlehill, the Commissary of Caithness, papers from 1696 until 1701. [NRS.NRAS.65.box 6-7]

CAMPBELL, MALCOLM, Chamberlain of Harris, [Na Hearadh], from 1703 until 1705. [TGSI.XLIV.314]

CAMPBELL, WILLIAM, M.A., minister at Bower, [Bagair], Caithness, from 1641 until 1649. [F.VII.114]

CAMPBELL, WILLIAM, the sheriff clerk of Caithness, a letter dated 16 October 1694. [NRS.GD112.39.168.13,]

CANRONACH, JOHN, in Dunballoch, Wardlaw, testament, 28 November 1630, Comm. Inverness. [NRS]

CHALMER, or GALD, in Dores, [Dubhras], Inverness-shire, testament, 13 January 1669, Comm. Inverness. [NRS]

CHAPMAN, JANET, spouse of John Stewart a bailie of Inverness, testament 27 February 1667, Comm. Inverness. [NRS]

CHAPMAN, ROBERT, a councillor of Inverness on 20 April 1644. [IMB.182]

CHISHOLM, [AN SIOSALACH], ALEXANDER, baron of Beauly, [A'Mhanachainn], Inverness-shire, was granted various lands in the parishes of Cullicuddin [Cul a Chudainn] and Conveth] An Confhadhach] which formerly pertained to the late Sir James Fraser of Bray, [Braigh], on 4 March 1659.
[RGSS.X.685]

CHISHOLM, ALEXANDER, of Comer, a witch-finder in the parishes of Kilmorack, [Cill Mhoraig], and Kiltarlity, [Cill Targhlain], Inverness-shire, in 1662. [TGSI.IX.118]

CHISHOLM, ALEXANDER, was described as an ill-affected and malicious neighbour of Inverness on 19 March 1666.
[IMB.228]

CHISHOLM, ALEXANDER, baillie to Lord Lovat, on 13 June 1681. [IMB.293]

CHISHOLM, DUNCAN, settled in York, Scarborough, Maine, by 1667. [LLNV.252]

CHISHOLM, JOHN, of Kinnerres, Kilterlity, [Cill Targlain], testament, 12 June 1630, Comm. Inverness. [NRS]

CHISHOLM, THOMAS, the younger, in Kilmorack, Inverness-shire, in 1673. [IR.24.80]

CHISHOLM, THOMAS, in Dornoch, Sutherland, paid his Hearth Tax in 1694. [NRS.E69.23.1.3]

CHISHOLM, MURDOCH, in Dornoch, Sutherland, paid his Hearth Tax in 1694. [NRS.E 69.23.1.3]

CLERK, DONALD, a cremer [pedlar], complained to the Inverness burgh council that some hucksters were selling goods at the Cross on the basis they were militia-men and were entitled to trade there, on 18 December 1671. [IMB.250]

CLERK, JOHN, in Inverness on 25 October 1667. [IMB.233]

CLARK, THOMAS, in Borlum, Abertarff, [Obar Thairbh], testament 7 December 1669, Comm. Inverness. [NRS]

CLUNES, ABRAHAM, from Ross-shire, a student at King's College, Aberdeen, in 1661. [KCA]

CLUNES, PATRICK, from Ross-shire, a student at King's College, Aberdeen, in 1658. [KCA]

CLUNES, WILLIAM, a shipmaster in Cromarty and his spouse Helen Hill, a sasine in 1700. [NRS.RS37.6.258]

COOK, MARGARET, spouse of Donald McLean in Leys, [An Leigheas], testament, 12 November 1689, Comm. Inverness. [NRS]

CORBAT, HECTOR, from Ross-shire, a student at King's College, Aberdeen, in 1660. [KCA]

CROOKSHANK, JOHN, in Auchnahanat, testament, 25 March 1678, Comm. Inverness. [NRS]

COUY, JOHN, a burgess of Inverness, testament, 15 July 1668, Comm. Inverness. [NRS]

COWIE, JAMES, was appointed as Lieutenant of a Militia Company, to protect Inverness from McDonald of Keppoch and his rebels, 3 September 1688. [IMB.7]

COWIE, JOHN, was appointed to negotiate with Skipper Richie regarding the prices, lengths, breadth, thickness, and strength of the timber required for the new bridge, on 4 July 1664. [IMB.219]

CROMBIE, WILLIAM, on 29 November 1647, was accused of deserting the town of Inverness 'in the time of the troubles'. [IMB.195]

CULLODEN, ALEXANDER, a skipper in Inverness in 1681. [RPCS.XI.530]

CUMMING, ALEXANDER, minister of Halkirk, [Hacraig], Caithness, and a burgess of Inverness, son of Jasper Cumming, deceased, 8 June 1625. [NRS.GD23.3.9]; a charter of salmon fishing in the River Ness, dated 8 March 1626. [NRS.GD23.3.10]

CUMMING, ALEXANDER, son of David Cumming of Duthil, [Daothal], Inverness-shire, a student at King's College, Aberdeen, in 1672. [KCA]

CUMMING, DAVID, Procurator Fiscal of Inverness, took the Test Oath on 19 December 1681. [IMB.299]

CUMMING, GEORGE, failed to appear before the High Burgh Court of Inverness on 10 January 1603. [ICB.3]

CUMING, GEORGE, a merchant in Inverness, testament 21 March 1666 Comm. Inverness. [NRS]

CUMMING, GEORGE, born 1627, son of Alexander Cumming of Tomnamoon, Moray, graduated MA from King's College, Aberdeen, in 1647, a schoolmaster in Elgin, Moray, minister of Urray and Tarradale, [Ross-shire], from 1658 until his death in 1705, husband of Janet Dunbar. [F.7.49]

CUMMING, GEORGE, was appointed Treasurer of Inverness for 1676-1677, on 26 September 1676; a councillor on 15 March 1680. [IMB.270/283]; Burgh Treasurer took the Test Oath on 19 December 1681. [IMB.299]

CUMING, JAMES, from Inverness, a student at King's College, Aberdeen, in 1676. [KCA]

CUMMING, JAMES, an apothecary and surgeon in London, died in Inverness, probate 1697, PCC. [TNA]

CUMMIN, JOHN, from Inverness, a student at King's College, Aberdeen, in 1665. [KCA]

CUMMING, MARGARET, a debtor for the stent in Kirk Street, Inverness, in 1647. [IMB.194]

CUMMING, ROBERT, of Relugas, [Ruigh Lugais], Moray, a merchant in Inverness, was admitted as a burgess and guilds-brother of Inverness on 20 June 1687. [IMB.7]

CUMMING, WILLIAM, eldest son of Alexander Cumming a burgess of Inverness, in debt to James Ross of Merkinch, [Marc Innis], Inverness, was imprisoned for eight weeks but escaped by 12 February 1648. [IMB.197]

CUMMING, WILLIAM, schoolmaster of the Grammar School of Inverness, on 26 January 1662. [IMB.214]

CUMMING, WILLIAM, a Sergeant of the Inverness Militia on 25 May 1665. [IMB.216]

CUMMING, WILLIAM, was described as an ill-affected and malicious neighbour of Inverness on 19 March 1666. [IMB.228]

CUMMING, ..., widow of George Cumming, in Inverness on 25 October 1667. [IMB.233]

CUTHBERT, ALEXANDER, failed to appear before the High Burgh Court of Inverness on 10 January 1603. [ICB.3]

CUTHBERT, ALEXANDER, a councillor of Inverness on 20 April 1644. [IMB.182]; former baillie and presently Dean of Guild of Inverness by 29 April 1653. [IMB.206]; Provost on 28 September 1670. [IMB.238]; testament 15 December 1680 Comm. Inverness. [NRS]

CUTHBERT, ALEXANDER, from Inverness, a student at King's College, Aberdeen, in 1671. [KCA]

CUTHBERT, ALEXANDER, eldest son of the deceased James Cuthbert, was admitted as a burgess and guild-brother of Inverness on 20 September 1686. [IMB.344]

CUTHBERT, ALEXANDER, son of the deceased David Cuthbert former Town Clerk of Inverness, was admitted as a burgess and guilds-brother of Inverness on 20 September 1686. [IMB.344]

CUTHBERT, DAVID, town clerk of Inverness, reference on 31 March 1642. [IMB.129]; a bond dated 26 August 1661. [NRS.RD3.2.326]

CUTHBERT, DAVID, a writer [lawyer] in Inverness, was appointed Deputy Town Clerk there on 19 December 1681. [IMB.298]; took the Test Oath on 19 December 1681 [IMB.299]

CUTHBERT, DAVID, second son of Provost John Cuthbert of Inverness, was admitted as a burgess and guilds-brother of Inverness on 20 September 1686. [IMB.344]

CUTHBERT, GEORGE, a merchant in Inverness, a bond dated 16 July 1661. [NRS.RD3.1.519]

CUTHBERT, GEORGE, of Castlehill, a juryman in an inquest in Inverness on 23 March 1686. [IMB.343]

CUTHBERT, ISOBEL, spouse of JOHN Hepburn a baillie of Inverness, testament 10 June 1668 Comm. Inverness. [NRS]

CUTHBERT, JAMES, the younger, failed to appear before the High Burgh Court of Inverness on 10 January 1603. [ICB.3]

CUTHBERT, JAMES, Provost of Inverness, was admitted as a burgess of Aberdeen on 17 February 1624. [ABR]

CUTHBERT, JAMES, of Draikies, [Dreigidh], Inverness, was appointed by the Committee of the Estates to negotiate with the Scots factors in Veere, Holland, re 150,000 guilders worth of arms and provision to be purchased there, on 10 December 1640, [IMB.176]; late bailie of the burgh of Inverness in 1676. [TGSI.4.172]

CUTHBERT, JAMES, son of Laurence Cuthbert, was ordered to find a house in Inverness suitable for the accommodation of schoolchildren, on 7 August 1665. [IMB.222]

CUTHBERT, JAMES, of Draikies, Inverness, the younger, a bond dated 7 August 1661. [NRS.RD4.3.5]

CUTHBERT, JAMES, town clerk of Inverness, testament 28 January 1680, Comm. Inverness. [NRS]

CUTHBERT, JAMES, second son of James Cuthbert, Ensign of the Inverness Militia on 25 May 1665. [IMB.216]; was admitted as a burgess and guilds-brother of Inverness on 20 September 1686. [IMB.344]; late baillie, took the Test Oath on 19 December 1681. [IMB.299]

CUTHBERT, JANET, spouse of Donald Buy in Inverness, testament 23 April 1669 Comm. Inverness [NRS]

CUTHBERT, JOHN, the younger, failed to appear before the High Burgh Court of Inverness on 10 January 1603. [ICB.3]

CUTHBERT, JOHN, of Castlehill, reference on 31 March 1642. [IMB.129]; was appointed Captain of the Inverness militia sent to Stratherick, [Srath Eunaraig], to support Lord Lovat opposing the Irish rebels in Glengarry, [Gleann Garadh], on 19 August 1644, on 23 August 1644 he was ordered to go to Badenoch, [Baideanach], Inverness-shire, where the rebels were looting and burning settlements. [IMB.184]

CUTHBERT, JOHN, of Wester Draikies, Inverness-shire, reference on 31 March 1642. [IMB.129]

CUTHBERT, JOHN, from Inverness, a student at King's College, Aberdeen, in 1665-1669. [KCA]; applied to become schoolmaster of Inverness, with success, on 20 September 1669. [IMB.237]

CUTHBERT, JOHN, a stent [tax] collector in Inverness on 19 April 1672. [IMB.252]; the elder, with twelve footmen, escorted eight seamen to Forres bound for Leith or Burntisland for service in the Royal Navy, on 27 April 1672, [IMB.253]; a juryman in an inquest in Inverness on 23 March 1686. [IMB.343]; was appointed a baillie of Inverness for 1676-1677, on 26 September 1676. [IMB.270]; was ordered to check the defences in Kirk Street, also the arms of every man there on 29 March 1679. [IMB.279]; a councillor on 15 March 1680. [IMB.283], a baillie, took the Test Oath on 19 December 1681. [IMB.299]

CUTHBERT, JOHN, the elder, a merchant, was appointed as Captain of a Militia Company, to protect Inverness from McDonald of Keppoch, [A'Cheapach], and his rebels, 3 September 1688. [IMB.7]

CUTHBERT, LAURENCE, with land on the carse by the River Ness in 1655. [IMB.210]

CUTHBERT, MARGARET, spouse of William Baillie the elder, treasurer of Inverness, testament, 11 January 1669, Comm. Inverness. [NRS]

CUTHBERT, WILLIAM, Town Clerk of Inverness on 19 December 1681. [IMB.298]; took the Test Oath on 19 December 1681. [IMB.299]

CUTHBERT, WILLIAM, of Old Castlehill, of the Inverness Burgh Court on 10 January 1603. [ICB.3]

CUTHBERT, WILLIAM, son of Alexander Cuthbert in Inverness, was apprenticed to Samuel Guthrie, a litster, [dyer], in Edinburgh, on 10 April 1616. [EAR]

CUTHBERT, WILLIAM, Lieutenant of the Inverness Militia on 25 May 1665. [IMB.216]

CUTHBERT WILLIAM, a councillor of Inverness, took the Test Oath on 26 September 1682. [IMB.310]

DAETES, HENRY, from Cantray, [Canntra], near Inverness, a glover in Briel in the Netherlands, married Hester Wills, from Sandwich, England, in Leiden, the Netherlands, on 27 April 1605. [Leiden Marriage Register]

DALLAS, JOHN ROY, in Wester Urquhal, Inverness-shire, was subjected to a precept of poinding for payment of a bond due to James MacIntosh a merchant in Inverness, on 31 July 1690. [NRS.GD23.10.302]

DALLAS, JOHN, a writer [lawyer] in Fortrose, [A'Chanananiach], Easter Ross, versus Alexander Fraser of

Kinnaries, for payment of a debt of £478.18 shillings Scots, on 27 February 1700. [NRS.GD23.10.400]

DALLAS, LILLIAS, spouse of Gregor Grant in Kerroger, Urquhart, testament, 22 November 1630, Comm. Inverness. [NRS]

DALLAS, WILLIAM, Collector of the Mort-cloth money in Inverness in 1686. [IMB.7]

DALLAS, WILLIAM, a councillor, took the Test Oath on 19 December 1681. [IMB.299]; was appointed as Lieutenant of a Militia Company to protect Inverness from McDonald of Keppoch and his rebels, 3 September 1688. [IMB.7]

DAULING, JAMES, master of the Ann of Inverness from Inverness to Barbados in September 1716. [NRS.E508.10.6; AC9.702]

DAVIDSON, JOHN, a merchant on Skye, [An t-Eileen Sgitheanach], Inverness-shire, was granted a lease of herring fishing in 1668. [NRS.E55.13]

DAVIDSON, WILLIAM, graduated MA from St Andrews University in 1595, minister at Reay, [Rath], Caithness, about 1601, then at Farr, Sutherland, from 1603 until 1608. Husband of Agnes Blackadder. [F.VII.106]

DAVIDSON, WILLIAM, a minister in Ireland, then at Canisbay Caithness, from 1652 until transferred to Birsay in 1666. [F.VII.116]

DEAN, DAVID, miller at Culloden, testament, 6 October 1676, Comm. Inverness. [NRS]

DEAS, DONALD, was responsible for hand-bell services in Inverness on 2 September 1682. [IMB.308]

DEMPSTER, ALEXANDER, in Dornoch, Sutherland, paid his Hearth Tax in 1694. [NRS.E69.23.1.3]

DEMPSTER, JOHN, minister at Creich, [Craoich], Sutherland, before 1664, then at Lairg, [Luirg], Sutherland, from 1668 until his death in 1705. In 1689 he was deprived for not praying for King James VII. [F.7.93]

DEMPSTER, JOHN, in Dornoch, Sutherland, paid his Hearth Tax in 1694. [NRS.E69.23.1.3]

DEMPSTER, THOMAS, in Dornoch, Sutherland, paid his Hearth Tax in 1694. [NRS.E69.23.1.3]

DENOON, DONALD, from Caithness, a student at King's College, Aberdeen, in 1667. [KCA]

DENUNE, WILLIAM, from Ross-shire, a student at King's College, Aberdeen, in 1646. [KCA]

DICK, JOHN, a pricker of witches in Tain, [Baile Dhubhthaich], Easter Ross, in 16.... [TGSI.IX.120]

DICK, JOHN, a cordiner [shoemaker] in Inverness on 25 October 1667. [IMB.233]; testament 18 March 1669 Comm. Inverness. [NRS]

DICK, MARGARET, spouse of William Dick a shoemaker in Castlehill, Inverness, testament, 29 September 1680, Comm. Inverness. [NRS]

DINGWALL, MARGARET, and Bessie Merchant, bakers had their oven removed on council orders due to it being a fire risk, on 9 September 1678. [IMB.279]

DOUGLAS, ANDREW, the Vicar of Inverness, failed to appear before the High Burgh Court of Inverness on 10 January 1603. [ICB.3]

DOUGLAS, or DALGLEISH, GEORGE, born 1681, son of Colin Douglas and his wife Elizabeth Irvine in the Diocese of Ross, was a student at the Scots College in Rome from 1698, probably ordained as a Catholic priest in 1707. [RSC.124]

DOUGLAS, JOHN, failed to appear before the High Burgh Court of Inverness on 10 January 1603. [ICB.3]

DOUGLAS, Dame MARGARET, Lady Alexander, was granted various lands in Inverness-shire on 27 August 1652. [RGSS.X.17]

DOULL, [DOMHNALL], JAMES, the elder in Wick, Caithness, testament dated 1623. [NRS.CC4.8.1]

DOUN, ALLISTER, in Abriachan, [Obar Bhritbeachan], Inverness-shire, the hangman on 27 November 1654. [IMB.210]

DOW, [DUBH], GORMELL, an alleged witch in Inverness in 1662. [TGSI.IX.119]

DOW, MURELL, an alleged witch in Inverness in 1662. [TGSI.IX.119]

DOW, WILLIAM a debtor for the stent in Inverness in 1647. [IMB.194]

DUFF, [DUBH], ALEXANDER, of Drumoore, was appointed as Commissioner for Inverness at the forthcoming Convention of Royal Burghs in Edinburgh on 5 July 1688.
[IMB.7]

DUFF, ANDREW, second son of William Duff a baillie of Inverness, was admitted as a burgess and guilds-brother of Inverness on 20 September 1686. [IMB.345]

DUFF, HUGH, from Ross-shire, minister at Fearn, [Manachainn Rois], Ross-shire, from 1696 until his death on 3 July 1739. [F.VII.56]

DUFF, JAMES, a Notary Public in Inverness in 1642. [IMB.181]

DUFF, RONALD, a Corporal of Monro's Company in Danish Service around 1628. [SAA.II.125]

DUFF, WILLIAM, a stent [tax] collector on 19 April 1672, [IMB.252]; a former bailie of Inverness, on 9 April 1679. [NRS.AC7.5]; was appointed a baillie of Inverness for 1676-1677, on 26 September 1676, also on 15 March 1680. [IMB.270/283]; , took the Test Oath on 19 December 1681. [IMB.299]

DUFF, WILLIAM, from Ross-shire, a student at King's College, Aberdeen, in 1670. [KCA]

DUFF, WILLIAM, the younger, a councillor of Inverness, took the Test Oath on 26 September 1682. [IMB.310]

DUFF, WILLIAM, Provost of Inverness in 1690s. [NRS.1150; 56/97]

DUFFUS, Lord ALEXANDER, was granted various lands in Sutherland [Cataibh], which formerly pertained to John Sutherland of Kellis, on 9 June 1654. [RGSS.X.285]

DUNBAR, Mr ALEXANDER, was appointed a schoolmaster of Inverness Grammar School on 23 December 1650 in place of Mr Robert Forbes. [IMB.204]; he resigned on 30 January 1654 and was replaced by Alexander Fraser, son of Alexander Fraser a litster [dyer]. [IMB.208]

DUNBAR, ALEXANDER, a merchant in Inverness, testament, 25 April 1679, Comm. Inverness. [NRS]

DUNBAR, ALEXANDER, treasurer of Inverness on 24 June 1644. [IMB.183]; was appointed Provost of Inverness for 1676-1677, on 26 September 1676, a councillor on 15 March 1680. [IMB.270/283]; Provost of Inverness, took the Test Oath on 19 December 1681. [IMB.299]

DUNBAR, ARCHIBALD, of Barnmuckatie, Provost of Inverness, legacies from 1689 until 1702. [NRS.NRAS.65.box 6/6]

DUNBAR, GEORGE, schoolmaster of Inverness in 1685. [NRS.RD3.6277/79]

DUNBAR, GEORGE, in Dornoch, Sutherland, paid his Hearth Tax in 1694. [NRS.E69.23.1.3]

DUNBAR, JAMES, son of James Dunbar of Dunphail, [Dun Fail], and his wife Janet Carmichael, an antenuptial marriage contract with Margaret Monro, daughter of George Monro of Tarrell, [Tarail], Ross-shire, dated 16 December 1616. [NRS.GD248.162.8]

DUNBAR, JAMES, an officer in Danish Service who was killed in action at Breitenburg, Germany, in September 1627. [SAA.II.130]

DUNBAR, JAMES, from Ross-shire, a student at King's College, Aberdeen, in 1661. [KCA]

DUNBAR, JAMES, the elder, a merchant, was appointed as Captain of a Militia Company, to protect Inverness from

McDonald of Keppoch and his rebels, 3 September 1688.
[IMB.7]

DUNBAR, JAMES, a baillie, was to participate in the trial of witches in Inverness on 28 April 1662. [IMB.213]; a councillor, took the Test Oath on 19 December 1681. [IMB.299]

DUNBAR, JAMES, the Excise collector in Inverness, Wester Ross and Cromarty from 1690 until 1691. [NRS.NRAS.65.box 6/8]

DUNBAR, JAMES, a merchant in Inverness, trading with London on 15 July 1692, also in 1708. [NRS.AC7.9; AC9.302]

DUNBAR, JEAN, spouse of Malcolm Fraser of Culduthill, testament, 13 March 1668, Comm. Inverness. [NRS]

DUNBAR, JOHN, from Sutherland, a student at King's College, Aberdeen, in 1665. [KCA]

DUNBAR, MARGARET, spouse of Thomas Green a shoemaker in Inverness, testament, 1 May 1667, Comm. Inverness. [NRS]

DUNBAR, PATRICK, from Sutherland, a student at King's College, Aberdeen, in 1659. [KCA]

DUNBAR, Mr PATRICK, of Bowermadden, Caithness, participated in the saving and salvage of the Pelsor of Amsterdam in the Pentland Firth in 1706. [NRS.AC9.239]

DUNBAR, ROBERT, from Caithness, a student at King's College, Aberdeen, in 1665.
[KCA]

DUNBAR, ..., versus Patrick Forbes the Bishop of Caithness, a decreet dated 29 October 1672. [NRS.CS98.794]

DUNCAN, [DONNACHADH], GEORGE, was appointed as Lieutenant of a Militia Company, to protect Inverness from McDonald of Keppoch and his rebels, 3 September 1688. [IMB.7]

DUNCAN, WILLIAM, of Seasyde, was shipwrecked off Norway in 1631. [NRAS.NRAS.13.folder 18]

DUNDAS, Captain LAWRENCE, a gentleman of Caithness, Collector of the Assess for Caithness in 1653. [STC.175]

FAIRNE, ALEXANDER, a merchant in Inverness on 3 January 1679, sold his ship the <u>Samson of Inverness</u> to Alan Brigg, a shipmaster of Fraserburgh, Aberdeenshire. [NRS.AC7.5]

FARQUHAR, Mr ALEXANDER, of Toulay, a debtor in Inverness Tolbooth, was released having assigned his movables and land to his creditors, on 2 September 1672. [IMB.255]

FARQUHAR [FEARCHAR] VIC EWAN, CHRISTIAN, an alleged witch in Inverness in 1662. [TGSI.IX.119]

FARQUHAR, ROBERT, of Mownay, was granted the barony of Cromarty on 1 March 1655, also lands in Inverness, once in the hands of Sir Thomas Urquhart. [RGSS.X.400]

FERGUSON, ALEXANDER, brother of Ferguson of Invercauld, Aberdeenshire, was admitted as a burgess of Inverness in 1702. [NRS.NRAS.61.box 13/6]

FEARN, ALEXANDER, from Ross-shire, a student at King's College, Aberdeen, in 1661-1663. [KCA]

FEARN, DAVID, from Ross-shire, a student at King's College, Aberdeen, in 1668. [KCA]

FINDLAY, ALEXANDER, in Dornoch, Sutherland, paid his Hearth Tax in 1694. [NRS.E69.23.1.3]

FINLAYSON, ALEXANDER, portioner of Culcairn, also a burgess of Inverness, testament, 13 December 1632, Comm. Inverness. [NRS]

FINDLAYSON, DONALD, a merchant burgess of Inverness, was fined forty merks and imprisoned for deserting the town 'during the late troubles'. [IMB.196]

FINDLAYSON, DONALD, from Ross-shire, a student at King's College, Aberdeen, in 1670. [KCA]

FINDLAYSON, JOHN, from Ross-shire, a student at King's College, Aberdeen, in 1661-1663. [KCA]

FINLAYSON, MARJORIE, spouse of George Hepburn a burgess of Inverness, testament, 17 June 1667, Comm. Inverness. [NRS]

FORBES, ALEXANDER, was described as an ill-affected and malicious neighbour of Inverness on 19 March 1666. [IMB.228]

FORBES, ALEXANDER, son of John Forbes of Culloden, was apprenticed to George Mossman a merchant in Edinburgh on 13 August 1673. [REA]

FORBES, ALEXANDER, claimed that he had been wrongly imprisoned in Inverness on 26 January 1674. [IMB.256]

FORBES, ALEXANDER, in Cullerny, Petty, testament, 8 February 1688, Comm. Inverness. [NRS]

FORBES, DONALD, a juryman in an inquest in Inverness on 23 March 1686. [IMB.343]; was appointed as Captain of a Militia Company, to protect Inverness from McDonald of Keppoch and his rebels, 3 September 1688. [IMB.7]

FORBES, DUNCAN, was described as an ill-affected and malicious neighbour of Inverness on 19 March 1666. [IMB.228]

FORBES, DUNCAN, from Inverness, a student at King's College, Aberdeen, in 1663. [KCA]; Provost of Inverness on 20 April 1644, [IMB.182]; a merchant in Inverness co-owner of the Dolphin on 3 January 1679. [NRS.AC7.5]

FORBES, FINLAY, a wright in Petty, [Peitidh], Inverness, in 1682. [SHS.24.114]

FORBES, JAMES, was appointed Captain of the Inverness contingent of the Scottish Army, on 17 March 1650. [IMB.204]

FORBES, JOHN, Provost of Inverness, a stent [tax] collector in Inverness on 30 August 1647, [IMB.193]; was granted lands in Sutherland formerly held by William Mackay of Bighouse, on 7 February 1653. [RGSS.X.85]

FORBES, JOHN, was described as an ill-affected and malicious neighbour of Inverness on 19 March 1666. [IMB.228]

FORBES, JOHN, son of John Forbes of Culloden, [Cuil Lodair], Inverness-shire, was apprenticed to James Graham a merchant in Edinburgh on 25 September 1678. [REA]

FORBES, ROBERT, applied for the post of schoolmaster of Inverness Grammar School on 17 July 1648, was appointed by 1 April 1650. [IMB.202/203]

FORBES, THOMAS, third son of John Forbes of Culloden, [Cuil Lodair], Inverness, was admitted as a burgess and guilds-brother of Inverness on 20 September 1686. [IMB.345]

FOULLAR, DAVID, rented a croft beyond the Water of Ness, formerly occupied by the late Francis Bishop, on 20 March 1665. [IMB.222]

FOWLER, DAVID, the elder, with twelve footmen, escorted eight seamen to Forres, Moray, bound for Leith or Burntisland for service in the Royal Navy, on 27 April 1672, [IMB.253]; a juryman in an inquest in Inverness on 23 March 1686. [IMB.343]; a merchant in Inverness, trading with London on 15 July 1692. [NRS.AC7.9]

FOULLAR, DONALD, the elder, a merchant burgess of Inverness, husband of Janet Robertson, and their son Donald, were accused, by George Abraham a baillie of Inverness, of using faulty weights for sixteen years, on 2 August 1641. [IMB.177]; was appointed stent [tax] collector for the East Gait of Inverness on 14 December 1644. [IMB.186]; he was granted the right to the anchorage fees from Michaelmass 1647 to Michaelmass 1648, also for 1648-1649. [IMN.195/198]; he was suspended from office of baillie on 29 April 1653 for opposing the power of the Dean of Guild. [IMB.208]

FOULLAR, DONALD, a councillor of Inverness, took the Test Oath on 26 September 1682. [IMB.310]

FRASER, AGNES, daughter of Hugh Fraser of Belladrum, and wife of John McKenzie of Applecross, Wester Ross, was granted a sasine of lands and settlements in the Barony of Applecross, [Abar Crosain], on 31 July 1649. [NRS.GD23.10.35]

FRASER, ALEXANDER, of Farraline, testament, 31 August 1630, Comm. Inverness. [NRS]

FRASER, or FRISSELL, Captain ALEXANDER, born in Lovat, Inverness-shire, residing in Den Haag, the Netherlands, testaments 21 March 1626 and 16 June 1628, refer to Andrew Fraser in Inverness. [GAR.ONA.28.81.217; 128.196.522]

FRASER, ALEXANDER, or MACWHARRAN, a merchant burgess of Inverness, son of the baron, was selected to join the army at Elgin, Moray but refused to go. Consequently, his burgess rights were withdrawn on 20 April 1644. [IMB.183]

FRASER, ALEXANDER, a Quartermaster of Fraser's Dragoons in 1644, during the Wars of the Three Kingdoms.

FRASER, ALEXANDER, of Tyre, a student at King's College, Aberdeen, in 1647. [KCA]

FRASER, ALEXANDER, son of Alexander Fraser a litster [dyer], was appointed schoolmaster of the Inverness Grammar School on 30 January 1654. [IMB.208]

FRASER, ALEXANDER, of Philorth, [Inverness-shire], the younger, was admitted as a burgess and guilds-brother of Edinburgh on 4 March 1663. [REB]

FRASER, ALEXANDER, a smith in Inverness, testament, 10 October 1667, Comm. Inverness. [NRS]

FRASER, ALEXANDER, from Inverness, a student at King's College, Aberdeen, in 1670. [KCA]

FRASER, ALEXANDER, miller at the King's Mill and at Deirbocht Mill, Inverness, was fined and imprisoned for using faulty measures on 30 October 1671. [IMB.249]

FRASER, ALEXANDER, minister at Daviot, [Deimhidh], Inverness, a bond dated 25 June 1674, [NRS.RD2.37.543]

FRASER, ALEXANDER, a skinner in Inverness, was subject to fraud by William McFrench and George Waus, on 28 June 1675. [IMB.263]

FRASER, ALEXANDER, of Beaufort, Inverness-shire, a student at King's College, Aberdeen, in 1678. [KCA]

FRASER, A., a councillor of Inverness on 15 March 1680. [IBM.283]

FRASER, ALEXANDER, minister at Petty, [Peitidh], Inverness, a deed in 1685. [NRS.RD3.61.521]

FRASER, ALEXANDER, of Kinnaries, Strathglass, Inverness-shire, was educated at Douai, France, from 1663, an apostate in Kiltarlity, [Cill Targhlain], Inverness-shire, in 1679, was liberated in Inverness in 1690. [NRS.GD23.10.226] [RPCS.15.178]

FRASER, Mr ALEXANDER, eldest son of the deceased James Fraser a burgess of Inverness, was admitted as a burgess and guild-brother of Inverness on 20 September 1686. [IMB.344]

FRASER, ALEXANDER, Collector of the Bishop's rents in Caithness, [Gaillaibh], a petition of 1710. [NRS.AC10.96]

FRASER, ANDREW, a clerk of the Diocese of Ross, also a Notary Public, a sasine by Andrew Denune of Little Hilltown, as bailie to Andrew Monro in Tain, attorney to , McIntosh, relict of George Ross of Balnagown, [Baile nan Gobhainn] now wife of Mr John Munro of Fearne, of lands in the barony of Ganyes, witnesses were George Monro of Tarrell, George Monro of Tarbat, John Munro of Lymlair, Alexander Baillie of Dunzean, Andrew Monro of Coulnard, John Monro of Pittonachtie, and Hector Monro of Fyndon, on 10 July 1615. [SRS.Munro of Foulis Writs]

FRASER, ANDREW, a merchant in Warsaw, Poland, in 1613, in Stockholm, Sweden, by 1616, father of Bernard [Berndt] Fraser, factor in Lubeck, Germany, for the Duke of Courland in 1646. [SG.13.4.]

FRASER, ANDREW, the Commissary of Inverness, was admitted as a burgess and guilds-brother of Aberdeen on 25 October 1632. [ABR]

FRASER, ANDREW, a burgess of Inverness, testament, 10 January 1633, Comm. Inverness. [NRS]

FRASER, ANDREW, from Inverness, a student at King's College, Aberdeen, in 1672-1673-1677. [KCA]

FRASER, ANDREW, was shipped, possibly via Inverness, to Pennsylvania by Morris Trent a merchant, then indentured before the Court of Quarter Sessions in Chester County, Pennsylvania, in September 1695. [SG.29.1.11]

FRASER, ANNA, daughter of Alexander Fraser, the Master of Lovat, and spouse of Alexander McKenzie of Applecross, [Aber Crosain], Wester Ross, a deed dated 29 January 1674. [NRS.RD2.36.672]

FRASER, DANIEL, a mariner on HMS Coventry probate 1699 Prerogative Court of Canterbury. [TNA]

FRASER, DAVID, second son of Finlay Fraser the Dean of Guild in Inverness was admitted as a burgess and guild-brother of Inverness on 20 September 1686. [IMB.344]

FRASER, DONALD, born 1620, son of William Fraser a minister at Kiltarlity, [Cill Targhlain], Inverness, graduated MA from King's College, Aberdeen, in 1637, minister at Kilmorack, [Cill Mhoraig], Inverness, from 1641 until 1664, later at Urquhart, Inverness-shire, from 1665 until his death on 5 October 1684, husband of Katherine Fraser. [F.7.46]

FRASER, DONALD, a prisoner in Edinburgh, was transported via Leith by Morris Trent a merchant, aboard the Mary bound for Barbados on 4 May 1663. [ECA; 186.13.4]

FRASER, DONALD, in Dalcross, [Dealgros], testament, 16 October 1666, Comm. Inverness. [NRS]

FRASER, DONALD, of Drummond, [An Duimein], Inverness-shire, probably bribed the jailers at Inverness to enable him to escape, 6 February 1674. [IMB.257]

FRASER, DONALD, a maltman in Inverness, testament, 31 August 1678, Comm. Inverness. [NRS]

FRASER, EDMOND, in Barbados, administration dated 1649, Prerogative Court of Canterbury. [TNA]

FRASER, FINLAY, a bailie of Inverness in 1662. [TGSI.IX.119]; was to participate in the trial of witches in Inverness on 28 April 1662. [IMB.213]; a baillie on 28 September 1670. [IMB.238]; was appointed a baillie of Inverness for 1676-1677, on 26 September 1676, also on 15 March 1680. [IMB.270/283]; took the Test Oath on 19 December 1681. [IMB.299]

FRASER, FREDERICK, a tailor in Inverness, testaments, 10 May and 19 July 1676, Comm. Inverness.
[NRS]

FRASER, Lieutenant Colonel HUGH, was admitted as a burgess and guilds-brother of Aberdeen on 12 September 1640, Colonel of Fraser's Dragoons from 1643 until 1647 during the Wars of the Three Kingdoms, [ABR]

FRASER, HUGH, of Clunvachy, the younger, a Lieutenant in Colonel Cranston's Regiment in the service of the King of Poland in 1656. [CF.417]

FRASER, HEW, Master of Lovat, Inverness-shire, was admitted as a burgess and guilds-brother of Aberdeen on 5 September 1642, [ABR]; as Lord Fraser of Lovat, granted a tack [lease] to his chamberlain James Lundie, of the lands and baronies of Abertarff, Stratherick, Beauly, in Strathglass, Inverness-shire, on 8 May 1668. [NRS.GD176.250]

FRASER, HEW, of Culbockie, [Cuil Bhocaidh], Ross-shire, a debtor in Inverness Tolbooth, was released having paid his creditors, on 19 December 1672. [IMB.255]

FRASER, HEW, a writer in Inverness, a bond dated 22 June 1674. [NRS.RD4.35.330]

FRASER, HUGH, of Fanblair, testament, 2 July 1678, Comm. Inverness. [NRS]

FRASER, HUGH, born 1643, son of Reverend Alexander Fraser in Petty, [Peitidh], Inverness-shire, graduated MA from King's College in Aberdeen in 1662, minister in Kiltarlity, [Cill Targhlain], and Glen Convinth, [An Confhadhach], Inverness-shire, from 1667 until his death in 1712, husband of Anna Murray. [F.VI.469]

FRASER, HUGO, of Belladrum, Inverness-shire, a servant of Lord Lovat, was admitted as a burgess and guilds-brother of Aberdeen on 31 August 1634. [ABR]

FRASER, HUCHEON, of Culbockie, Wardlaw, Inverness, testament, 11 March 1634, Comm. Inverness. [NRS]

FRASER, JAMES, a burgess of Inverness, testament, 24 October 1666, Comm. Inverness. [NRS]

FRASER, JAMES, [1634-1709], minister at Wardlaw, Inverness, theological papers. [NRS.NRAS1098]

FRASER, JAMES, of Pitkellian, [Baile a Choillein], Ross-shire, a prisoner in Inverness Tolbooth on 14 June 1686. [IMB.344]

FRASER, JAMES, master of the Joan of Inverness trading between Findhorn, [Inbhir Eireann], Moray, and Holland in 1689-1691. [NRS.E72.11.15/16/18/19]

FRASER, JANET, spouse of Donald McWilliam in Monyack, [Mon Itheig], Inverness-shire, testament, 18 June 1677, Comm. Inverness. [NRS]

FRASER, JOHN, son of the laird of Dores, [Dubhras], Inverness-shire, was admitted as a burgess of Aberdeen on 3 September 1602. [ABR]

FRASER, JOHN, failed to appear before the High Burgh Court of Inverness on 10 January 1603. [ICB.3]

FRASER, JOHN, from Ross-shire, a student at King's College, Aberdeen, in 1659. [KCA]

FRASER, JOHN, a ship's carpenter aboard the Conclusion which was captured by the Turks on the return voyage from Barbados and then imprisoned in Algiers in 1679. [RPCS.VII.152]

FRASER, JOHN, in Croy, testament, 15 July 1680, Comm. Inverness. [NRS]

FRASER, JOHN, a smith and keeper of the Inverness burgh clock, on 14 November 1681. [IMB.298]

FRASER, JOHN, of Pitculzean, [Baile a' Choillein], Ross-shire, a Covenanting minister, was banished to the Plantations then transported via Leith aboard the Henry and Francis bound for East New Jersey in September 1685, landed on 7 December 1685, later minister at Woodbury, Connecticut, returned to Scotland around 1688, died in Alness, Ross and Cromarty on 7 November 1711. [F.7.26/663] [RPCS.11.154/289/292] [NWI.1.422] [ETR.368]

FRASER, JOHN, the elder, a merchant, was appointed as Captain of a Militia Company, to protect Inverness from McDonald of Keppoch and his rebels, 3 September 1688. [IMB.7]

FRASER, JOHN, was admitted to the Scots Charitable Society of Boston, New England, in 1690. [NEHGS/SCS]

FRASER, JOHN, a skipper in Inverness, a deed in 1693, [NRS.RD4.72.1254]; master of the Adventure of Inverness trading between Inverness and Rotterdam, Bergen in Norway, and London between 1682 and 1683. [NRS.E72.11.5/6/7/8]; master of the Joan of Inverness trading between Inverness and Rotterdam, Holland, in 1690, master of the Amity of Inverness trading between Findhorn, Moray, and Holland in 1691. [NRS.E72.18/19]

FRASER, JOHN, from Thurso, Caithness, returned from Virginia to Scotland in 1690. [Edinburgh City Records, August 1690]

FRASER, JOHN, was shipped to Pennsylvania then indentured before the Court of Quarter Sessions in Chester County, Pennsylvania, on 14 December 1698. [SG.29.1.13]

FRASER, JOHN, a mariner aboard the Mary of London, died at Guinea, probate, 1700 Prerogative Court of Canterbury. [TNA]

FRASER, JOHN, a minister who emigrated to Virginia in 1701, a curate in Northumberland, Va., and later in King George parish, died in Pitscataway, Maryland in November 1742. [EMA.28][FPA.35]

FRASER, KATHERINE, spouse of Farquhar Cuming in Little Inshbrine, Urquhart, Inverness, a bond dated 31 October 1661. [NRS.RD4.3.497]

FRASER, LILIAS, spouse of Lauchlan Fraser in Fanellan, testament, 9 February 1667, Comm. Inverness. [NRS]

FRASER, MALCOLM, of Clytelle Feris, Inverness, testament, 11 March 1634, Comm. Inverness. [NRS]

FRASER, MARGARET, spouse of Angus McIntosh in Drummond, [Druimein], Inverness-shire, a testament, 21 April 1679, Comm. Inverness. [NRS]

FRASER, MARJORIE, spouse of William McPhail in Tullochgorm, testament, 2 August 1679, Comm. Inverness. [NRS]

FRASER, MARIE, spouse of Alexander Fraser a burgess of Inverness, testament, 18 May 1669, Comm. Inverness. [NRS]

FRASER, Mr MICHAEL, applied to become schoolmaster of Inverness, without success, on 20 September 1669. [IMB.237]

FRASER, MOIR, spouse of John McFerquhair Vic Ean, in Overchalador, a tack, dated 9 November 1674. [NRS.RD4.36.94]

FRASER, Sir PETER, of Dores, [Dubhras], Inverness-shire, a letter to William Mill a writer [lawyer] in Dundee, dated 16 July 1698. [NRS.RH9.2.108]

FRASER, PETER, surgeon aboard the Lucy of London, died at sea when bound for the West Indies, probate 1695 Prerogative Court of Canterbury. [TNA]

FRASER, PETER, was educated at the Scots College in Paris from 1696 to 1702, was ordained at Scothouse on 11 March 1704, a Roman Catholic priest in Strathaven, Banffshire in 1710, died in Morar, Inverness-shire on 9 March 1731. [NRS.CH1.2.30/1.5][SCP.212][IR.IV.206]

FRASER, ROBERT, a cramer [pedlar], complained to the burgh council of Inverness that some hucksters were selling goods at the Burgh Cross on the basis they were militia-men and were entitled to trade there, on 18 December 1671. [IMB.250]

FRASER, ROBERT, and his wife Anne, in Albemarle County, North Carolina, on 10 August 1694. [NCSA.SS.978.1/62]

FRASER, RORIE, a cramer [pedlar] in Inverness on 1 August 1670. [IMB.242]

FRASER, SIMON, Lord Lovat, from Inverness-shire, was admitted as a burgess of Aberdeen on 14 August 1619. [ABR]

FRASER, SIMON, in Kulmaskiak, an apostate in Kiltarlity, [Cill Targhlain], Inverness-shire, in 1679. [IR.24.82]

FRASER, THOMAS, entered the Swedish Army under Sir James Spens of Wormiston in 1606, father of Andrew [Anders] Fraser, born 1616, a Major in the Swedish Army, died in 1686. [SG.13.4.23]

FRASER, THOMAS, of Knockie, failed to appear before the High Burgh Court of Inverness on 10 January 1603. [ICB.3]

FRASER, THOMAS, of Moniack, [Mon Itheig], Inverness-shire, failed to appear before the High Burgh Court of Inverness on 10 January 1603. [ICB.3]

FRASER, THOMAS, son of James Fraser in Inverness in 1643. [IMB.193]

FRASER, THOMAS, of Tain, [Baile Dhubhthaich], Easter Ross, a student at King's College, Aberdeen, in 1659. [KCA]

FRASER, THOMAS, a Lieutenant in Danish Service in Copenhagen in 1658. [RAK]

FRASER, THOMAS, a servant to Sir Alexander Fraser of Dores, [Dubhras], Inverness-shire, a royal physician, was admitted as a burgess and guilds-brother of Edinburgh on 18 December 1668. [REB]

FRASER, THOMAS, probably from Inverness-shire, was educated at Marischal College, Aberdeen, in 1659, schoolmaster at Kirkhill, Inverness in 1677. [MCA.11.226] [Inverness and Dingwall Presbytery Records.78]

FRASER, THOMAS, in Lovat, testament, 26 June 1677 Comm. Inverness. [NRS]

FRASER, THOMAS, a merchant in Inverness, was appointed as Captain of a Militia Company, to protect Inverness from McDonald of Keppoch and his rebels, 3 September 1688. [IMB.7]

FRASER, THOMAS, from Dores, [Dubhras], Inverness-shire, a chaplain who died aboard HMS Suffolk, probate 1694, Prerogative Court of Canterbury. [TNA]

FRASER, THOMAS, a mariner in Inverness in 1708. [NRS.AC9.314]

FRASER, THOMAS, the younger, a merchant in Inverness in 1708. [NRS. AC9.302]

FRASER, W., a soldier of the 2nd Company of Cockburn's Regiment in Swedish Service in 1609. [SIS.217]

FRASER, Mr WILLIAM, in the Kirk of Kilmorack, [Cill Mhoraig], Inverness-shire, a servant of Lord Lovat, was admitted as a burgess and guilds-brother of Aberdeen on 31 August 1634. [ABR]

FRASER, WILLIAM, of Culbokie, [Cuil Bhocaidh], Ross-shire, a servant of Lord Lovat, was admitted as a burgess and guilds-brother of Aberdeen on 31 August 1634. [ABR]

FRASER, WILLIAM, from Ross-shire, a student at King's College, Aberdeen, in 1661. [KCA]

FRASER, WILLIAM, in Barbados by 1683. [SPAWI.1683.1365]

FRASER, WILLIAM, second son of the late Alexander Fraser a smith burgess of Inverness, was admitted as a burgess and guilds-brother of Inverness on 27 September 1686. [IMB.7]

FRASER, WILLIAM, a skipper, son of Rorie Fraser a merchant in Inverness, was admitted as a burgess and guild-brother of Inverness on 20 September 1686. [IMB.344]; master of the Alexander of Inverness trading between Inverness and Rotterdam, Holland, and London between 1685 and 1691, [NRS.E72.11.10/11/12/13/14/15/16/18/19]; his ship was wrecked and looted in the Moray Firth, before 10 August 1705, [NRS.AC8.57]; testament dated 4 June 1718, Comm. Inverness. [NRS]

FRASER, WILLIAM, a merchant in Inverness, versus John Findlay and others in 1700. [NRS.AC8.58]; in 1708, [NRS.AC9.302/306]

FRASER, WILLIAM, settled in Henrico County, Virginia, by 1700. [CAG.I.562]

FRASER, ..., a bailie of Inverness, was ordered to check the defences in Bridge Street and 'beyond the water', also the arms of every man there on 29 March 1679. [IMB.279]

FRISSELL, ALEXANDER, settled in New England around 1660. [LLNV.253]

FRISELL, ALEXANDER, was buried in St Peter's parish, Barbados, in 1679. [H2.89]

FRISSELL, ALEXANDER, was shipped from Scotland to Pennsylvania, possibly by William Trent in Inverness, then indentured for six or seven years in Chester County, Pa., on 14 December 1698. [SG.29.1.13]

FRIZELL, DANIEL, a soldier of Lieutenant Colonel Thomas Lewis' Company in Barbados on 6 January 1679. [H2.101]

FRISELL, DAVID, a mariner aboard HMS Essex, probate 1692 Prerogative Court of Canterbury. [TNA]

FRIZELL, EDWARD, probably from Inverness-shire, was captured at the Siege of Worcester in 1651, was transported via London aboard the John and Sarah to New England in November 1651, landed in Boston in February 1652. [Suffolk Deeds, 1-56]

FRISELL, GEORGE, was admitted to the Scots Charitable Society in Boston in 1686. [SCS]

FRISELL, JOHN, was admitted to the Scots Charitable Society in Boston in 1686. [SCS]

FRISSELL, THOMAS, a corporal of John Monro of Assynt's Company in Danish Service in 1628. [SAA.II.125]

FRIZELL, WILLIAM, probably from Inverness-shire, was captured at the Siege of Worcester in 1651, was transported via London aboard the John and Sarah to New England in November 1651, landed in Boston in February 1652. [Suffolk Deeds, 1-56]

FRIZELL, WILLIAM, a Scotsman in Herefordshire, probate 1696 Prerogative Court of Canterbury. [TNA]

GAIR, [GEARR], ALEXANDER, in Pitcalnie, [Baile Chailnidh], Ross-shire, and his eldest son Thomas Gair, purchased lands in Nigg, [An Uig], Ross-shire, with the consent of his mother Agnes Hossack and his wife Isabel McKenzie, on 24 March 1668. [NRS.GD1.48.3]

GAIRE, THOMAS, a chapman, was elected a councillor of Cromarty in 1669. [RPCS.3.III]

GARY, WILLIAM, in Dell, testament, 11 January 1676, Comm. Inverness. [NRS]

GEDDES, WILLIAM, a shipmaster in Inverness, brought timber from Norway for the new bridge at Inverness on 4 July 1664, [IMB.219]; on 18 December 1691. [NRS.AC7.9]; master of the David of Inverness in 1664, of the Fortune of Inverness in 1665, and the Alexander of Inverness, trading with Rotterdam, Holland, from 1681. Deeds from 1665 until 1682, [NRS.RD2/RD3/RD4]; Captain William Geddes, a skipper in Inverness on 18 December 1691. [NRS.AC7.9]

GEORGESON, ANDREW, from Caithness, a student at King's College, Aberdeen, in 1663. [KCA]

GER, THOMAS, from Ross-shire, a student at King's College, Aberdeen, in 1663. [KCA]

GIBSON, ALEXANDER, born 1630 son of John Gibson in Edinburgh, graduated MA from Edinburgh University in 1652, minister at Bower, [Bagair], Caithness, from 1659 until 1692. Husband of Katherine Sinclair, parents of Alexander, John, Archibald, George, and Elizabeth. [F.VII.114]

GLAS, JANET, in Dornoch, Sutherland, paid her Hearth Tax in 1694. [NRS.E69.23.1.3]

GLASS, JOHN, in Dornoch, Sutherland, paid his Hearth Tax in 1694. [NRS.E69.23.1.3]

GLASH, [GLAS], DONALD, a shoemaker, leased land beyond Altnaskiach, Sutherland, was to be sold on 11 May 1688. [IMB.7]

GOLLANE, GEORGE, a burgess of Rosemarkie, deceased, late resident near Rosemarkie, [Ros Mhaircnidh], Easter Ross, in 1654. [RGSS.X.356]

GOLLANE, ROBERT, a burgess of Rosemarkie, deceased, late near Rosemarkie, [Ros Mhaircnidh], Easter Ross, in 1654. [RGSS.X.356]

GORDON, ALEXANDER, from Sutherland, a student at King's College, Aberdeen, in 1669 [KCA]

GORDON, BESSIE, in Dornoch, [Dornach], Sutherland, paid her Hearth Tax in 1694. [NRS.E69.23.1.3]

GORDON, GEORGE, of Sutherland, a student at King's College, Aberdeen, in 1648. [KCA]

GORDON, GEORGE, Collector of the Poll Tax money in Sutherland, o 30 June 1696. [NRS.E70.17.31]; also, Collector of the Hearth Tax in Dornoch, Sutherland, in the 1690s. [NRS.E69.23.1.3]

GORDON, Mr GILBERT, a servant of John, the Earl of Sutherland, wa admitted as a burgess of Aberdeen on 22 April 1624. [ABR]

GORDON, JAMES, a mason in Inverness on 4 July 1664. [IMB.219]

GORDON, JANET, in Dornoch, Sutherland, paid his Hearth Tax in 1694. [NRS.E69.23.1.3]

GORDON, JOHN, from Ross-shire, a student at King's College, Aberdeen, in 1665. [KCA]

GORDON, JOHN, son of William Gordon a burgess of Dornoch, was apprenticed to James Sutherland a merchant in Edinburgh on 23 September 1657. [REA]

GORDON, JOHN, ['Jan Gordeijn'], a soldier from Sutherland, aboard the Eendracht bound for the Dutch East Indies in 1668. [GAR.ONA.239.11.22]

GORDON, JOHN, Lord Strathnaver, from Sutherland, raised his regiment in 1689.

GORDON, JOHN, of Embo, [Earabol], Sutherland, a Captain of Strathnaver's Regiment in 1689.

GORDON, JOHN, in Dornoch, Sutherland, paid his Hearth Tax in 1694. [NRS.E69.23.1.3]

GORDON, RICHARD, failed to appear before the High Burgh Court of Inverness on 10 January 1603. [ICB.3]

GORDON, Sir ROBERT, Tutor of Sutherland, was admitted as a burgess of Aberdeen on 20 September 1619. [ABR]

GORDON, WILLIAM, Inverness burgh agent on 9 April 1677. [IMB.272]

GOW, WILLIAM, a merchant in Wick, Caithness, a bond by James Muir, a merchant in Meldrums Haugh, for £258, 15 shillings, written by James Young a merchant in Wick, Caithness, and witnessed by Hugh Harrower, a merchant in Wick, on 31 March 1697. [NRS.NRAS.3215, bundle 24-25]

GOWIN, [GOBHAINN], MARIE, an alleged witch in Inverness in 1662. [TGSI.IX.119]

GRAHAM, ALEXANDER, of Drynie, Provost of Fortrose, [A'Chananaich], Ross-shire, Commissioner to the Convention of Royal Burghs on 14 July 1676. [IMB.268]

GRAHAM, ROBERT, deceased, sometime Dean of Ross, late resident near Rosemarkie, [Ros Mhaircnidh], Easter Ross, in 1654. [RGSS.X.356]

GRAHAM, WILLIAM, a burgess of Inverness, testament, 30 August 1634, Comm. Inverness. [NRS]

GRANT. ALEXANDER, a merchant in Inverness, testament, 9 January 1668, Comm. Inverness. [NRS]

GRANT, ALEXANDER, of Kellintrae, testament 7 July 1678, Comm. Inverness. [NRS]

GRANT, DONALD, of Inverladnan, testament 19 July 1676 Comm. Inverness. [NRS]

GRANT, ELSPET, spouse of William McConachie of Rathemoon, testament Comm. Inverness 19 October 1680. [NRS]

GRANT GRISSELL, spouse of Sweine Grant in Bellintoune, testament 30 August 1666 Comm. Inverness. [NRS]

GRANT, ISABEL, spouse of James Butteraugh, in Granish, Duthill, testament 25 March 1678 Comm. Inverness. [NRS]

GRANT, JAMES, a burgess of Elgin, Moray, natural son of the deceased George Grant, a burgess of Inverness, was legitimised on 10 March 1658. [RGSS.X.645]

GRANT, JAMES, in Innerlednan, Duthill, testament 3 September 1666, Comm. Inverness. [NRS]

GRANT, JOHN, son of John Grant of Garthinbeg, Duthill, testament, 6 December 1632 Comm. Inverness. [NRS]

GRANT, JOHN, on 29 November 1647, was accused of deserting the town of Inverness 'in the time of the troubles'. [IMB.195]

GRANT, KATHERINE, spouse of Finlay Grant in Culnakirk, Urquhart, testament 16 November 1630 Comm. Inverness. [NRS]

GRANT, MARIE, spouse of John McFinlay in Bunloid, Urquhart, testament 26 March 1668 Comm. Inverness. [NRS]

GRANT, MUNGO, of Kinchirdiem testament 18 October 1680 Comm. Inverness. [NRS]

GRANT, NEIL, born 1684, was transported from Scotland to Pennsylvania, possibly by William Trent a merchant in

Inverness, was brought before Bucks County Court in Pennsylvania, in September 1697. [SG.29.1.14]

GRANT, or MCCONACHY, PATRICK, in Kincherdie, testament 25 March 1678 Comm. Inverness. [NRS]

GRANT, ROBERT, a burgess of Channory, [A'Channanaich], Ross-shire, deceased, late resident near Rosemarkie, [Ros Mhaircnidh], Easter Ross, in 1654. [RGSS.X.356]

GRAY, ALEXANDER, of Espisdaill, was granted the town and lands of Tarlogie, [Tarlagaidh],Tain, Ross-shire, on 15 February 1656. [RGSS.X.504]

GRAY, CHRISTIAN, in Dornoch, Sutherland, paid his Hearth Tax in 1694. [NRS.E69.23.1.3]hilders

GRAY, JAMES, son of William Gray, minister at Lairg, Sutherland, in 1607, died in 1652, married [1] Janet McCulloch [2] Isabella McGill. [F.7.92]

GRAY, JOHN, a weaver and servant of Robert Irving in Drakies, Inverness-shire, testament 10 March 1680 Comm. Inverness. [NRS]

GRAY, ROBERT, son of Mr George Gray minister at Dornoch, was apprenticed to George Childers a saddler in Edinburgh on 23 September 1668. [REA]

GRAY, WILLIAM, 'the Provost's man', in Inverness on 25 October 1667. [IMB.233]

GROAT, DONALD and MALCOLM, of Waires, Caithness, a deed in 1697. [NRS.RD4.81.128]

GROAT, JOHN, of Duncansby, Caithness, the elder, a deed in 1694. [NRS.RD4.75.344]

GROUNDWATER, JOHN, possibly from Orkney, was transported from Scotland to Pennsylvania, possibly by William Trent a merchant in Inverness, was indentured for seven or eight years in Chester County, Pa., on 14 December 1698. [SG.29.1.13]

GUNN, ALEXANDER, of Killeirnan, [Cill Iurnain], Ross-shire, a deed in 1685. [NRS.RD2.66.433]

GUNN, [GUINNE], DANIEL, possibly from Sutherland, was captured at the Siege of Worcester in 1651, and transported via London aboard the John and Sarah to New England in November 1651, landed in Boston in February 1652. [Suffolk Deeds, 1-56]

GUNN, DANIEL, possibly from Sutherland a militiaman in Barbados in 1679. [H2/184]

GUNN, GEORGE, possibly from Sutherland, an officer of Mackay's Regiment in Danish Service from 1626, later in Swedish service in 1629. [TGSI.VIII.188][SAA.II.130]

GUNN, HENRY, whose sons Edward and Henry died in Hudson Bay Company Service before 1683. [HBRS.9.163/166]

GUNN, JOHN, born October 1608, an officer in Mackay's Regiment in Danish Service in 1626, in Swedish Service in 1629. [TGI.VIII.188]; a Colonel in Germany in the service of Gustavus Adolphus around 1630, Military Governor of Ohlua in Silesia from 1638 until his death on 9 April 1649. He was buried in the Evangelical church there. [SIG.283/316][MGIF.Map 3][SAA.II.130]

GUNN, JOHN, possibly from Sutherland, a soldier of 2nd Company of Cockburn's Regiment in Swedish Service in 1609. [SIS.217]

GUNN, JOHN, a soldier who was granted a pass to travel to Bergen in the Netherlands on 12 February 1620. [TNA.E157.86]

GUNN, JOHN, possibly from Sutherland, an officer of Mackay's Regiment in Danish Service in 1629. [TGSI.VIII.188]

GUNN, JOHN, in Virginia by 1654. [EVI]

GUNN, JOHN, possibly from Sutherland a militiaman In Barbados in 1679. [H2.159/184]

GUNN, JOHN, son of John Gunn of Navidaill, [Nemheadal], Sutherland, was apprenticed to Robert Gray, a saddler in Edinburgh on 8 February 1682. [REA]

GUNN, THOMAS, a mariner aboard HMS Elizabeth, died aboard HMS Victory, probate 1697 Prerogative Court of Canterbury. [TNA]

GUNN, WILLIAM, born 1597, a soldier who was granted a pass to travel to Rotterdam in the Netherlands on 15 December 1621. [TNA.E157.8]

GUNN, Sir WILLIAM, possibly from Sutherland, Captain of Mackay's Regiment in Danish Service in 1626, in Swedish Service in 1629, later Colonel of a Dutch Regiment. [TGSI.VIII.186]; a Colonel in Germany in the service of King Gustavus Adolphus of Sweden around 1630, later a General of the Imperial Army. [SIG.282][SAA.II.122]

GUNN, WILLIAM, in Elizabeth City County, Virginia, in 1635. [EVI]

HALL, JOHN, Excise Collector in Inverness on 3 January 1657. [IMB.7][NRS.AC2.1]

HARDY, THOMAS, in the Croft of Urlathrast, testament 28 April 1681 Comm. Inverness. [NRS]

HARPER, THOMAS, master of the Elizabeth of Inverness, arrived in Inverness on 28 August 1684 from London. [NRS.E72.11.8]

HARROW, ALEXANDER, a carpenter in Thurso, Caithness, participated in the saving and salvage of the Pelsor of Amsterdam in the Pentland Firth in 1706. [NRS.AC9.239]

HATMAKER, JOHN, imprisoned in Inverness Tolbooth in December 1684. [IMB.320]

HAY, ELSPET, spouse of James Grant of Achtherneik, testament 15 January 1676 Comm. Inverness. [NRS]

HAY, GEORGE, master of the Inverness Music School in 1689. [NRS.RD4.46.812]

HAY, JAMES, from Moray, [Moireibh], graduated MA from King's College, Aberdeen, in 1666, minister at Kildonan, Sutherland, from 1673 until his death in August 1705. [F.7.90]

HAY, JAMES, from Ross-shire, a student at King's College, Aberdeen, in 1676. [KCA]

HAY, JOHN, from Thurso, Caithness, returned to Scotland from Virginia in 1690. [Edinburgh Burgh Records, August 1690]

HAY, MARGARET, spouse to James Cuming a burgess of Inverness, testament 22 November 1630 Comm. Inverness. [NRS]

HAY, MARION, spouse of Finlay Gordon a cordiner in Inverness, testament 9 April 1635 Comm. Inverness. [NRS]

HENRIE, WILLIAM, a mason and burgess of Inverness, 1682. [SHS.24.114]

HEPBURN, JAMES, from Inverness, a student at King's College, Aberdeen, in 1667. [KCA]

HEPBURN, JOHN, a merchant burgess of Inverness, was authorised to collect stent money to build a Gaelic church in Inverness on 14 June 1648. [IMB.201]; was responsible for collecting anchorage and shore duty at Inverness from 1649 to 1650. [IMB.202]; was to participate in the trial of witches in Inverness on 28 April 1662. [IMB.213]; a baillie on 28 September 1670. [IMB.238]; took the Test Oath on 26 September 1682. [IMB.310]

HEPBURN, Sir ROBERT, of Keith, sold the lands and barony of Foulis, [Foghlais], in the parish of Kiltearn, Ross-shire, to Lauchlan McIntosh of Torcastle, [Tor a' Chaisteil], Inverness-shire, on 7 July 1674, witnesses were Andrew Oswald clerk of the Exchequer, Thomas Moncreiff clerk of the Exchequer, and William Broune presenter of signatures; notary was John Alexander. [SRS.Munro of Foulis Writs]

HEPBURN, ..., a bailiff, a juryman in an inquest in Inverness on 23 March 1686. [IMB.343]

HERCULES, JAMES, [Herkless?] was shipped from Scotland to Pennsylvania, possibly by William Trent in Inverness, then indentured in Chester County, Pa., on 14 December 1698. [SG.29.1.11]

HOBKIRK, ALEXANDER, a baxter, [baker], in Inverness, testament 23 February 1681 Comm. Inverness. [NRS]

HOGG, ROBERT, a seaman in Cromarty, husband of Katherine Skinner, a sasine in 1673. [NRS.RS36.5.207]

HOLM, DAVID, second son of the deceased James Holm a burgess of Inverness, was admitted as a burgess and guild-brother of Inverness on 20 September 1686. [IMB.344]

HOOMES, JAMES, in Inverness on 25 October 1667. [IMB.233]

HOME, WILLIAM, was appointed as Lieutenant of a Militia Company, to protect Inverness from McDonald of Keppoch and his rebels, on 3 September 1688. [IMB.7]

HOSSACK, ANDREW, in Inverness in 1643. [IMB.193]

HOSACK, CHRISTIAN, in Suddie, [Suidhe], Ross-shire, in 1652. [PID.247]

HOSSACK, DONALD, a ferrier in Cromarty, husband of Margaret Williamson, a sasine around 1696. [NRS.RS38.VI.436]

HOSSICK, JOHN, a mariner aboard the Josiah, who died at sea, probate1691 Prerogative Court of Canterbury. [TNA]

HOSSACK, SAMUEL, son of the deceased John Hossack a glover burgess of Inverness, was admitted as a burgess and guilds-brother there on 10 January 1687. [IMB.7]

HOSSACK, THOMAS, a fisherman in Cromarty, husband of Agnes Skinner, a sasine in 1690. [NRS.RS36.5.581]

HOSSACK, WILLIAM, a glover burgess of Inverness, testament 13 January 1669 Comm. Inverness. [NRS]

HOUSTON, Mr THOMAS, failed to appear before the High Burgh Court of Inverness on 10 January 1603. [ICB.3]

HOUTON, GEORGE, a skinner in Inverness, testament 13 January 1669 Comm. Inverness. [NRS]

HUNTER, DAVID, master of the Unity of Inverness, deeds in 1665-1666. [NRS.RD3.10.275; RD4.16.192]

IAN DUY VIC FINLAY, BAKIE, from Strathglass, Inverness-shire, an alleged witch in Inverness in 1662. [TGSI.IX.119-120]

IAN CHAIL, JANET, an alleged witch in Strathglass, Inverness-shire, was tried in Inverness in 1662. [TGSI.IX.119-120]

INNES, ARTHUR, from Sandside Caithness, a student at King's College, Aberdeen, in 1675. [KCA]

INNES, Mr JAMES, son of William Innis of Sandside, Caithness, was admitted as a burgess and guilds-brother of Aberdeen on 26 April 1647. [ABR]

INNES, JAMES, born 1638, graduated MA from Marischal College, Aberdeen, in 1666, minister at Canisbay, Caithness, from 1667 until his death on 24 December 1704. Husband of Jean Munro, parents of Theodore Innes a merchant in Edinburgh, James Innes who settled in South Carolina, and Barbara Innes, wife of John Sutherland, a merchant in Thurso. [F.VII.116]

INNES, JOHN, Clerk to the Kirk Session of Inverness in 1676. [TGSI.4.172]

INNES, JOHN, son of William Innes of Sandside, Caithness, an officer of Mackay's Regiment, was killed at Stralsund, Mecklenburg, Germany, in 16…. [TGSI.VIII.188]

INNES, JOHN, jailer in Inverness, was accused of allowing Alexander Blackwood access to the keys of the jail who then released James Moir a prisoner there, on 4 February 1667. [IMB.231]

INNES, JOHN, precentor, complained about what was being taught in the schools in Inverness, on 16 April 1677. Subsequently, bailie Rose inspected the Grammar School, while Hew Robertson, Andrew Shaw, and William Paterson, checked the unlicenced schools, including those at Rory Sinclair's, Isobel Fraser's, and George Anderson's houses, on 14 May 1677. [IMB.273]

INNES, PATRICK, a Captain in Danish Service, who was killed at Nurnberg in 1632. [SAA.II.130]

INNES, ROBERT, an officer in Danish Service in 1626-1627. [SAA.II.130]

INNES, ROBERT, from Caithness, a student at King's College, Aberdeen, in 1671. [KCA]

INNES, ROBERT, a merchant of Inverness, on 9 April 1679. [NRS.AC7.5]; was appointed as Captain of a Militia Company, to protect Inverness from McDonald of Keppoch and his rebels, on 3 September 1688. [IMB.7]; was granted the lands and barony of Delny, [Deilgnidh], Inverness-shire, on 10 February 1653. [NRS.GD1.125.3]

INNES, WALTER, of Inverbrecky, [Inbhir Breacaidh], Ross-shire, disposed of land in the barony of Deny, Ross-shire, to his son Walter Innes, on 19 February 1688. [NRS.GD1.187.12]

IRVINE, ALEXANDER, of Crimond, Aberdeen, was admitted as a burgess of Inverness around 1705. [NRS.NRAS.1500, box 588]

JENOR, ELSPET, spouse of Alexander Allan in Dalcorse, [Dealgros], testament 11 March 1670 Comm. Inverness. [NRS]

JOHNSTONE, ALEXANDER, a seaman in Cromarty, husband of Janet Skinner, a sasine around 1685. [NRS.RS.36.5.208]

JOHNSTONE, JOHN, in Thurso, [Inbhir Theorsa], Caithness, in 1658. [RGSS.X.634]

JUNCKEN, MICHAEL, a burgess of Inverness, testament 21 July 1668 Comm. Inverness. [NRS]

KEALLOCH, JAMES, master of the <u>Elizabeth of Inverness</u>, trading between Inverness and Rotterdam, Holland, Norway, and London in 1685 to 1686. [NRS.E2.11.10/11/12/13]

KEILLOCH, WILLIAM, a juryman in an inquest in Inverness on 23 March 1686. [IMB.343]; a councillor took the Test Oath on 19 December 1681. IMB.299]; was appointed as a Lieutenant of a Militia Company, to protect Inverness from McDonald of Keppoch and his rebels, 3 September 1688. [IMB.7]

KERONACH, FARQUHAR, in Mullochard, testament 25 March 1678 Comm. Inverness. [NRS]

KERR, JOHN, at the Inverness Burgh Court on 10 January 1603. [ICB.3]

KING, JOHN, reader and master of the Music School in Inverness, , testament 6 May 1670 Comm. Inverness. [NRS]

KINROSS, CHARLES, a servant of the Earl of Cromarty in 1707. [NRS.AC9.253]

LAMBIE, WILLIAM, master of the <u>Adventure of Inverness</u> trading between Rotterdam, Holland, and Inverness in 1683. [NRS.E72.11.7]

LAUDER, JAMES, graduated MA at Edinburgh University in 1592, minister at Avoch, [Abhach], Ross-shire, from 1607 until 1642. [F.VII.1]

LAUDER, WILLIAM, born 1614, son of Reverend James Lauder, graduated MA from King's College, Aberdeen, in 1632, minister at Avoch, Ross-shire, from 1642 until 1660s. [F.VII.1]

LAW, JOHN, a skipper in Cromarty, a deed in 1673. [NRS.RD4.34.277]

LEITCH, ALEXANDER, a saddler in Dornoch, [Dornach], Sutherland, husband of Eva Weir, a sasine dated 20 August 1623. [NRS.GD1.498.10]

LEITH, GEORGE, a burgess of Inverness, son and heir of Alexander Leith, on 12 December 1665. [NRS.GD1.498.16]

LESLY, GEORGE, graduated MA from King's College, Aberdeen, minister at Bower, [Bagair], Caithness, from 1637, died by 1664. Father of Harry. [F.VII.114]

LESLY, GEORGE, Sheriff Clerk of Inverness on 12 June 1645. [IMB.189]; testament 4 December 1678 Comm. Inverness. [NRS]

LILLIE, FRANCIS, a pilot and master of the <u>Hopewell of Inverness</u>, versus William MacWhirrie and Thomas Alves, merchants in Inverness for freight due for a voyage to Danzig, in 1712. [NRS.AC8.145]

LINDSAY, DAVID, from Cromarty, a student at King's College, Aberdeen, in 1674. [KCA]

LOCKHART, JOHN, a juryman in an inquest in Inverness on 23 March 1686. [IMB.343]

LORIMER, THOMAS, failed to appear before the High Burgh Court of Inverness on 10 January 1603. [ICB.3]

LEUGACH, JANET, 'ane vile and wicked person', who had been banished from Inverness returned and was 'transgressing grossly during the time of divine service on the Lord's Day being drunk and vomiting in the High Church to the great dishonour of God and contempt of his Church', was to be whipped ten times on her bare back at the Tron then to be whipped six times in every street, and then banished from Inverness forever, 11 July 1681. [IMB.294]

LUNAN, WILLIAM, M.A., minister at Cromarty from 1638 until 1645. [F.VII.4]

LUNDSDAILL, BEATRIX, spouse of John Shaw of Gusslich, , testament 13 January 1676 Comm. Inverness. [NRS]

MACAINE, FINLAY VIC AINE, servant of John Lowson, was banished from Inverness for one year for escaping from the burgh tolbooth, on 22 November 1602. [ICB.3]

MACALLAN, JOHN, a burgess of Inverness, confirmed that he had received 100 pounds from George McConnell Reoch, on 11 December 1602. Witnesses were Findlay McVirrich, Alexander Skinner, John MacVirrich, burgesses of Inverness, and Alexander Duff, Notary Public, and Town Clerk, [ICB.3]; failed to appear before the High Burgh Court of Inverness on 10 January 1603. [ICB.3]

MCALLAN, MURDO, in Belchroan, testament 3 September 1666 Comm. Inverness. [NRS]

MCALLISTER, DONALD, with Mary his wife, and son John, apostates in Comar, Kiltarlity, Inverness-shire, in 1679. [IR.XXIV.82]

MACALLISTER VICCONNELL DOWY, DUNCAN, from Urray, Ross-shire, admitted participating in the Royalist uprising led by James Graham, Marquis of Montrose into England and at the Siege of Inverness in 1649. [SHS.24.181][NRS.CH2.92.1]

MCALLISTER, JOHN DOW, failed to appear before the High Burgh Court of Inverness on 10 January 1603. [ICB.3]

MCALLISTER, THOMAS MCCANDY, in Delnahatnich, Duthill, testament 8 July 1633 Comm. Inverness. [NRS]

MCALLISTER, THOMAS vic BREBER, in Aberchallader, testament 6 May 1668 Comm. Inverness. [NRS]

MCALLISTER, THOMAS, from Castle Kilcohee, Inverness, settled in St Lucy's parish in Barbados, probate dated 24 March 1684, Barbados.

MCANDREW, ANGUS, a miller in Kythmitly, testament 3 September 1666 Comm. Inverness. [NRS]

MCANDREW, JOHN, in Conage, [A'Chonnis], Petty, Inverness-shire, testament 1 October 1677 Comm. Inverness. [NRS]

MCANE, BEAN, in Cullachie, Abertarff, [Obar Thairbh], testament 18 October 1630 Comm. Inverness. [NRS]

MCANEROCH, WILLIAM, in Farraline, testament 16 August 1630 Comm. Inverness. [NRS]

MACASKELL, ALLAN, possibly from Skye, [An t-Eilean Sgitheanch], Inverness-shire, a soldier of Captain Davie's Company of Militia in Barbados in 1679. [H2.109]

MACASKELL, DANIEL, possibly from Skye, Inverness-shire, a soldier of Captain Davie's Company of Militia in Barbados in 1679. [H2.109]

MACASKILL, DONALD, in St John's parish, Barbados, probate dated 15 March 1710, Barbados.

MACASKEY, ALLAN, with 1 servant, 2 freemen, and 25 slaves, on 17 acres in the parish of St Joseph, Barbados, in 1680. [H2.26]

MACAULAY, [MACKULLO], ANDREW, in Tain, [Baile Dhubhthaich], Ross-shire, was admitted as a burgess of Aberdeen on 2 September 1629. [ABR]

MACAULAY, HUGH, imprisoned in Edinburgh Tolbooth, was released to go to Holland as a soldier in 1689. [RPCS.XIII.573]

MACAULAY, [MACKULLO], JOHN, in Tain, [Baile Dhubhthaicj], Ross-shire, was admitted as a burgess of Aberdeen on 2 September 1629. [ABR]

MACAULAY, THOMAS, residing in Inverness, was pursued in January 1603 by William Robertson the younger, a burgess of Inverness, for a debt of 20 merks due for two gallons of whisky supplied in January 1602. [ICB.4]

MACCHANDICH, NEIL, in Eigg, [Eige], Inverness-shire, in 1703. [NRS.CH1.2.5.2]

MACBANE, DONALD, born in 1663 near Inverness, a soldier from 1687 to 1716, fought in various European campaigns, died after 1728. Author of 'The Expert Swordman's Companion, [Glasgow, 1728]

MCBAIN, ANGUS, from Inverness, a student at King's College, Aberdeen, in 1671. [KCA]

MCBEAN, ANGUS, a messenger in Inverness, eldest son of the deceased Andrew McBean a burgess there, a juryman in an inquest in Inverness on 23 March 1686. [IMB.343]; was admitted as a burgess and guilds-brother of Inverness on 27 September 1686. [IMB.345]

MCBEAN, BEAN, of Tomatin, [Tom Aitinn], testament 20 July 1666 Comm. Inverness. [NRS]

MCBEAN, DONALD, of Faylie, gave a bond of forty merks Scots towards the construction of the bridge at Inverness, on 10 July 1682. [IMB.305]

MCBEAN, GILLIES, of Little Draikies, [Dreigidh], Inverness-shire, gave a bond of one hundred merks Scots towards the construction of the bridge at Inverness, on 10 July 1682. [IMB.305]

MCBEAN, JOHN, late master of the burgh weigh-house of Inverness was reinstated on 3 April 1648. [IMB.198]

MCBEAN, JOHN, from Inverness, a student at King's College, Aberdeen, in 1669. [KCA]

MCBEAN, JOHN, in the Old Town of Clava, [Clabhlag], testament 5 June 1676 Comm. Inverness. [NRS]

MCBEAN, JOHN, in Bellinloan, [Baile an Loin], Inverness,-shire, son of William McBean the elder in Bellinloan, a burgess of Inverness, was admitted as a burgess and guilds brother of Inverness on 27 September 1686. [IMB.345]; a merchant in Inverness, deeds in 1697. [NRS; RD2.80.2.628; RD4.80.1024; RD4.81.1419]

MCBEAN, KATHERINE, relict of Angus Shaw of Tordarroch, testamer 1 March 1678 Comm. Inverness. [NRS]

MCBEAN, WILLIAM, was reimbursed for expenses involved in repairing the dock at Inverness on 23 May1670. [IMB.242]

MCBEAN, WILLIAM, a stent [tax] collector in Inverness on 19 April 1672. [IMB.252]; a juryman in an inquest in Inverness on 23 March 1686. [IMB.343]; took the Test Oath on 19 December 1681. [IMB.29

MCCHATICH, ALEXANDER, a seaman in Inverness, testament 15 February 1633 Comm. Inverness. [NRS]

MCCHEILL, JOHN, in Kingussie, testament 8 September 1666 Comm Inverness. [NRS]

MCCLACHAR, THOMAS BEGG, in Urray or Kilchrist, [Cille Chriosd], Ross-shire, participated in the rebellion under James Graham, Marquis of Montrose, in 1649. [SHS.24.159]

MCCLAY, DAVID, in Holme, [An Tuilm], Inverness, testament 20 November 1667 Comm. Inverness. [NRS]

MCCLAY, JOHN, in Croy, [Crothaigh], testament 10 January 1668 Comm. Inverness. [NRS]

MCCLERICH, ALEXANDER, in Nudbeg, Kingusie, [Ceann a'Ghiuthsaicl testament 1 November 1630 Comm. Inverness. [NRS]

MCCLERICH, SYMON, in Belladern, Conveth, [An Confhadhach], testament 4 April 1633 Comm. Inverness. [NRS]

MCCOIL, ALEXANDER, with his family, in the Kirkton of Comar, Kiltarlity, Inverness-shire, in1710. [NRS.CH1.2.29.3]

MCCOIL, DONALD, with his family of six, in the Kirkton of Comar, Kiltarlity, Inverness-shire, in 1710. [NRS.CH1.2.29.3]

MCCOIL DOWIE, JOHN, in Guisachan, Kiltarlity, Inverness-shire, in 1710. [NRS.CH1.2.29.3]

MCCOILE, DUNCAN, in Erchit, [Earchoighd], Inverness], testament, 21 April 1679. Com. Inverness. [NRS]

MCCOIL, NIEL, in Morar, Inverness-shire, in 1703. [NRS.CH1.2.5.2]

MCCOILE, WILLIAM, in Bellinlon, testament, 12 June 1677, Comm. Inverness. [NRS]

MCCOLL, or MCBEAN, DONALD OIG, in Balloan, [Baile an Loin], Inverness-shire, was subjected to a precept of poinding for payment of a bond due to James MacIntosh a merchant in Inverness, on 31 July 1690. [NRS.GD23.10.302]

MCCOMAS, DONALD, in Inverness in 1643. [IMB.193]

MCCOMAS, THOMAS, in Moy, Inverness, testament, 10 May 1634, Comm. Inverness. [NRS]

MCCOMIE, ALEXANDER, in Mussadinan, Boleskin, [Both Fhleisginn], testament, 18 June 1632, Comm. Inverness. [NRS]

MCCOMYE, [MACCOMAIDH], JOHN, a servant of Lord Lovat, Inverness-shire, was admitted as a burgess and guilds-brother of Aberdeen, on 13 March 1635. [ABR]

MCCOMYES, JOHN, a servant of the Earl of Seaforth, was admitted as a burgess and guilds-brother of Aberdeen on 4 April 1637. [ABR]

MACCONCHIE, ALEXANDER, failed to appear before the High Burgh Court of Inverness on 10 January 1603. [ICB.3]

MCCONCHIE, ALEXANDER, was authorised to grant licenses to Highlanders and to residents of Inverness permitting them to sell whisky within Inverness-shire, on 25 May 1663. [IMB.215]

MCCONACHY, ANGUS, a skinner in Inverness, testament, 7 December 1632, Comm. Inverness. [NRS]

MCCONCHIE, DUGAL, in Breacharnoy, Glengarry, [Gleann Garadh], Morar, Inverness-shire, in 1703. [NRS.CH1.2.5.2]

MCCONACHY, JANET, spouse of Donald Paterson a webster, [weaver], in Inverness, testament, 7 December 1632, Comm. Inverness. [NRS]

MCCONACHY, JOHN, a merchant burgess of Inverness, testament, 28 August 1669, Comm. Inverness. [NRS]

MCCONCHIE, METTIE, was authorised to grant licenses to Highlanders and to residents of Inverness permitting them to sell whisky within Inverness-shire, on 25 May 1663. [IMB.215]; spouse of William Monro a skinner and cordiner, [shoemaker], burgess of Inverness, testament, 1 September 1669, Comm. Inverness. [NRS]

MCCONCHIE, WILLIAM, in Inverness on 25 October 1667. [IMB.233]

MCCONNELL, AGNES, spouse of William McEwan a caird, [craftsman], in Cloyne, Conveth, [An Confhadhach], testament, 16 May 1633, Comm. Inverness. [NRS]

MCCONNELL, ANDREW FRASER, failed to appear before the High Burgh Court of Inverness on 10 January 1603. [ICB.3]

MCCONNELL, ANGUS GORME, took goods from a ship of Leith at Barra, [Barraigh], in the Outer Hebrides, bound from Glasgow to Danzig, a discharge was granted by Walter Stirling, a merchant burgess of Glasgow, on 6 December 1627. [NRS.GD201.1.18]

MCCONNELL, Sir DONALD, of Sleat, [Skleite], Inverness-shire, and his eldest son James, a contract with Sir John McKenzie of Tarbert, [An Tairbeart], Ross-shire, and his sister Margaret McKenzie, dated 23 February 1633. [NRS.GD305.1.127-128]

MCCONNELL VICEAN RIACH, DUNCAN, in Urray, [Urrath], or Kilchrist, Ross-shire, took part in the in rebellion under James Graham, Marquis of Montrose, in 1649. [SHS.24.159]

MCCONNELL, JAMES FRASER, failed to appear before the High Burgh Court of Inverness on 10 January 1603. [ICB.3]

MCCONNELL ROY, MCCONNELL VAINE, in Urray, [Urrath], or Kilchrist, Ross-shire, participated in the rebellion under James Graham, Marquis of Montrose, in 1649.
[SHS.24.159]

MCCONNELL DOWY VICWILLIAM, JOHN, in Urray , [Urrath], or Kilchrist, participated in the rebellion under James Graham, Marquis of Montrose, in 1649. [SHS.24.159]

MCCONNELL VCANGUS, THOMAS, in Forsinard, [Forsan Ard], Reay, [Rath], Sutherland, on 27 April 1640. [NRS.GD23.4.8]

MCCONNELL VAYNE VICEAN VEICK, WILLIAM, in Urray, [Urrath], or Kilchrist, Ross-shire, participated in the rebellion under James Graham, Marquis of Montrose, in 1649. [SHS.24.159]

MCCORMICK, DONALD, a debtor for the stent in Kirk Street, Inverness in 1647. [IMB.194]

MCCOULL, DONALD, in Dornoch, Sutherland, paid his tax in1694.NRSS.E69.23.1.3]

MCCOULL, ROBERT, failed to appear before the High Burgh Court of Inverness on 10 January 1603. [ICB.3]

MCCOULL, RORIE, a ship carpenter on the Green of Muirtown, [Baile an Fhraoich], Inverness, testament, 1 April 1677, Comm. Inverness. [NRS]

MCCOULL, WILLIAM, in Dornoch, Sutherland, paid his Hearth Tax in 1694. [NRS.E69.23.1.3]

MCCRAE, CHRISTOPHER, chamberlain to the laird of Comar, Inverness-shire, in 1703. [NRS.CH1.2.5.2]

MCCRA, JOHN, a periwig maker, to surrender his burgess rights as imprisoned for insulting William Dallas, the stent [tax] collector in December 1684. [IMB.320]

MCCULLOCH, CHARLES, son of Andrew McCulloch the Provost of Tain, was apprenticed to David Kennedy a surgeon in Edinburgh, on 19 October 1653. [REA]

MCCULLOCH, Mr DUNCAN, minister of the Gaelic church in Inverness, since 1643 complained to the Burgh Council that he had not received his annual stipend of 400 merks, a committee was set up to decide who should be taxed to finance the stipend on 14 July 1645. [IMB.189]

MCCULLOCH, GEORGE, was admitted as a burgess of Inverness on 27 December 1647. [IMB.196]

MCCULLOCH, GEORGE, in Dornoch, Sutherland, paid his Hearth Tax in 1694. [NRS.E69.23.1.3]

MCCULLOCH, HUGH, from Kingulloch, Golspie, [Goillspidh], Sutherland, a student at King's College, Aberdeen, in 1670. [KCA]

MCCULLOCH, JAMES, from Ross-shire, a student at King's College, Aberdeen, in 1667-1670. [KCA]

MCCULLOCH, JAMES, in Dornoch, Sutherland, paid his Hearth Tax in 1694. [NRS.E69.23.1.3]

MCCULLOCH, JOHN, son of Mr John McCulloh in Golspie, Sutherland, a student at King's College, Aberdeen, in 1676. [KCA]

MCCULLOCH, JOHN, in Dornoch, Sutherland, paid his Hearth Tax in 1694. [NRS.E69.23.1.3]

MCCULLOCH, ROBERT, from Ross-shire, a student at King's College, Aberdeen, in 1667. [KCA]

MCDONALD, ALEXANDER, brother-german of Sir Donald McDonald of Sleat, a marriage contract with Isobel McKenzie, sister of Alexander McKenzie, fiar of Gairloch, dated 23 January 1629. [NRS.NRAS.143.bundle 30]

MCDONALD, ALEXANDER, of Morar, Inverness-shire, accepted Oliver Cromwell as his overlord, a bond dated 12 March 1655 subscribed at Sconce near Inverness. [TGSI.14.74]

MCDONALD, ALEXANDER, possibly from Inverness-shire, married Catherine Woodhouse, in Christchurch, Barbados, on 26 May 1673. [PR]

MACDONALD, Sir ALEXANDER, a wadset for 5 penny lands of Ord, 3 penny lands of Crossovaig, 2 penny lands of Taskabaig, Skye, and 6 penny lands of Tarskabaig Mor, Skye, to Roderick Macdonald in Castletown, dated 1673. [TGSI.14.67]

MCDONALD, ALEXANDER, a tacksman took the 'Oath of the Friends' thereby undertaking to financially support the McDonalds of Skye, subscribed at Duntulm, [Dun Tuilm], Skye, on 1 February 1678. [TGSI.14.66]

MCDONALD, ALEXANDER, of Glengarry, [Gleann Garadh], Inverness-shire, letters between 1688 and 1710, [NRS.NRAS.65.box.8/1]; a Jacobite at the Battle of Killiecrankie, Perthshire, on 27 July 1689. [APS.IX.55]; deeds in 1694. [NRS.RD3.82.100; RD4.75.425]

MCDONALD, ALEXANDER, in Trotternish, [Trosaraidh], Skye, [An t-Eilean Sgitheanach], Inverness-shire, chamberlain to Sir Donald McDonald of Sleat, in 1703. [NRS.CH1.2.5.2]

MCDONALD, ALEXANDER, with his children – Donald, Alexander, Mary, Una, Margaret, Katherine [born 1700], and John [born 1701] – in Flodigeary, [Flodaigearraidh], Kilmory, Trotternish, Skye, Inverness-shire, in 1703. [NRS.CH1.2.5.2]

MCDONALD, ALLAN NIC COUL, of Morar, Inverness-shire, in 1703. [NRS.CH1.2.5.2]

MCDONALD, ALLAN, servant to the laird of Morar, Inverness-shire, in 1703. [NRS.CH1.2.5.2]

MCDONALD, ANGUS, of Glengarry, Inverness-shire, was admitted as a burgess and guilds-brother of Aberdeen on 5 September 1642, [ABR]; in Kirkibost, Bernera, [Bearnaraigh], in the Outer Hebrides, was appointed a Major General by King Charles II in 1655. [NRS.CH12.12.1865]; accepted Oliver Cromwell as his overlord, a bond dated 12 March 1655 subscribed at Sconce near Inverness. [TGSI.14.74]

MCDONALD, ANGUS, a tacksman in Kirkibost, Bernera, [Bearnaraigh], Outer Hebrides, took the 'Oath of the Friends' thereby undertaking to financially support the McDonalds of Skye, subscribed at Duntuilme, Skye, on 1 February 1678. [TGSI.14.66]

MCDONALD, ANGUS, with four children, in Belgarva, South Uist, in 1703. [NRS.CH1.2.5.2]

MCDONALD, ANGUS, in south west South Uist in 1703. [NRS.CH1.2.5.2]

MCDONALD, ANGUS, in Morar, Inverness-shire, brother of John McDonald in Suinsletter in 1703. [NRS.CH1.2.5.2]

MCDONALD, A., a tacksman took the 'Oath of the Friends' thereby undertaking to financially support the McDonalds of Skye, subscribed at Duntuilme, Skye, on 1 February 1678. [TGSI.14.66]

MCDONALD, COL, son of the deceased Archibald McDonald of Keppoch, [A' Cheapach] , Inverness-shire], was imprisoned in Inverness for failing to pay his cess tax, he claimed that as a minor he should not have been jailed and that he was a student at St Andrews University at the time, he was released subject to a penalty of one thousand pounds, on 10 February 1683. [IMB.313]

MCDONALD, DONALD, of Mundort, accepted Oliver Cromwell as his overlord, a bond dated 12 March 1655 subscribed at Sconce near Inverness. [TGSI.14.74]

MCDONALD, DONALD, a tacksman, took the 'Oath of the Friends' thereby undertaking to financially support the McDonalds of Skye, subscribed at Duntuilme, Skye, on 1 February 1678. [TGSI.14.66]

MCDONALD, DUNCAN, probably from Inverness-shire, a Jacobite soldier who was captured at the Battle of Cromdale, [Crombail], in Strathspey, [Srath Spe], on 1 May 1690. [RPCS.15.304]

MCDONALD, FLORENCE, daughter of Rorie McDonald, brother of Ronald McDonald of Benbecula, in the Outer Hebrides, and spouse of Angus McDonald son of Allan McDonald of Morar the elder, a marriage contract dated 3 April 1674. [NRS.RD2.37.233]

MCDONALD, H., a tacksman, took the 'Oath of the Friends' thereby undertaking to financially support the McDonalds of Skye, subscribed at Duntuilme, Skye, on 1 February 1678. [TGSI.14.66]

MCDONALD, Sir JAMES, of Sleat, Inverness-shire, accepted Oliver Cromwell as his overlord, a bond dated 12 March 1655 subscribed at Sconce near Inverness. [TGSI.14.74]

MCDONALD, J., a tacksman took the 'Oath of the Friends' thereby undertaking to financially support the McDonalds of Skye, subscribed at Duntuilme, Skye, on 1 February 1678. [TGSI.14.66]

MACDONALD, Sir JAMES, was confirmed in the lands of Trotternish, [Trondairnis], Skye, Inverness-shire, as heir to his father Sir Donald MacDonald, on 7 July 1654. [RGSS.X.297]

MCDONALD, JAMES, a tacksman took the 'Oath of the Friends' thereby undertaking to financially support the McDonalds of Skye, subscribed at Duntuilme on 1 February 1678. [TGSI.14.66]

MCDONALD, Sir JAMES, of McDonald, a tacksman took the 'Oath of the Friends' thereby undertaking to financially support the McDonalds of Skye, subscribed at Duntuilme on 1 February 1678. [TGSI.14.66]

MCDONALD MCALLAN VCEAN, JOHN, Captain of Clan Ranald, took goods from a ship of Leith at Barra in the Outer Hebrides, bound from Glasgow to Danzig, a discharge was granted by Walter Stirling, a merchant burgess of Glasgow, on 6 December 1627. [NRS.GD201.1.18]

MCDONALD, JOHN, of Stronewracke, accepted Oliver Cromwell as his overlord, a bond dated 12 March 1655 subscribed at Sconce near Inverness. [TGSI.14.74]

MCDONALD, JOHN, of Leik, Inverness-shire, and Finlay McDonald servant to Lord McDonald, arrived in Inverness on 28 August 1665 to negotiate a deal for joint defence, the council agreed subject to Clan Donald disarming their men. [IMB.225]; however, on 20 September the burgh council of Inverness, appealed to the Privy Council to send a troop of horse and 200 foot soldiers to garrison and defend the burgh. [IMB.225]

MCDONALD, JOHN, a tacksman in Griminess, [Griminis], Benbecula, Outer Hebrides, took the 'Oath of the Friends' thereby undertaking to financially support the McDonalds of Skye, subscribed at Duntuilme, Skye, on 1 February 1678. [TGSI.14.66]

MCDONALD, JOHN, of Beusdill, South Uist, in 1703. [NRS.CH1.2.5.2]

MCDONALD, JOHN, with two children in Dallborrou, South Uist, in 1703. [NRS.CH1.2.5.2]

MCDONALD, JOHN, in Suinsletter, Morar, Inverness-shire, in 1703. [NRS.CH1.2.5.2]

MCDONALD, J., a tacksman took the 'Oath of the Friends' thereby undertaking to financially support the McDonalds of Skye, subscribed at Duntuilme, Skye, on 1 February 1678. [TGSI.14.66]

MCDONALD, LACHLAN, in Eigg, Inverness-shire, in 1703. [NRS.CH1.2.5.2]

MCDONALD, RANALD, on Benbecula, [Beinn a Bhaghla], Outer Hebrides, accepted Oliver Cromwell as his overlord, in a bond dated 12 March 1655 subscribed at Sconce near Inverness. [TGSI.14.74]

MCDONALD, RANALD, of Gellovie, [Gallabaidh], Inverness-shire, a marriage contract with Isabel McIntosh, daughter of Angus McIntosh of Holme, dated 30 July 1691. Witnesses were Willam McIntosh of Borlum, Donald McIntosh of Kylachy, Alexander McPherson of Strathmassie, William Baillie of Dunain, William Baillie the Commissary of Inverness, Malcolm McIntosh in Dores, and James Baillie a writer [lawyer] in Inverness. [NRS.GD178.638]

MCDONALD, RANALD, in Trotternish, Skye, Inverness-shire, in 1703. [NRS.CH1.2.5.2]

MCDONALD, RANALD, of Kinbeathy, Trotternish, Skye, Inverness-shire, in 1703. [NRS.CH1.2.5.2]

MCDONALD, RANALD, of Cross, Morar, Inverness-shire, brother of Allan McDonald, in 1703. [NRS.CH1.2.5.2]

MCDONALD, RANALD, in Inverosy, Morar, Inverness-shire, in 1703. [NRS.CH1.2.5.2]

MCDONALD, RODERICK, a tacksman took the 'Oath of the Friends' thereby undertaking to financially support the McDonalds of Skye, subscribed at Duntuilme, Skye, on 1 February 1678. [TGSI.14.66]

MCDONALD, RONALD, of Keppoch, [A'Cheapach], Inverness-shire, a Jacobite soldier in 1689. [APS.app.ix.55]

MCDONALD, SOIRLE, with two children, in Gerriffliuch, South Uist, Outer Hebrides, in 1703. [NRS.CH1.2.5.2]

MCDONALD, ... of Auchterawe, [Uachdar Adha], Inverness-shire, a Jacobite soldier in 1689. [APS.app.ix.55]

MACDONELL, ALEXANDER, a Catholic in Ardnafouram, Arisaig, Inverness-shire, around 1701. [NRS.CH1.2.5.2]

MACDONELL, ALEXANDER, the younger, of Borradaill, [Borghdal], a Catholic in Arisaig, Inverness-shire, around 1701. [NRS.CH1.2.5.2]

MACDONELL, DONALD, of Wester Aberchalder, [Obar Chaladair], Glengarry, Inverness-shire, in 1703. [NRS.CH1.2.5.2]

MACDONELL, DONALD, of Lundie, Knoydart, [Cnoideart], Inverness-shire, in 1703. [NRS.CH1.2.5.2]

MCDONEL, HUBERT, was married in Bergen op Zoom, Brabant, on 5 April 1707. [WBA]

MCDONELL, JAMES, of Bellfinlay, Arisaig, Inverness-shire, in 1703. [NRS.CH1.2.5.2]

MACDONELL, JAMES, of Culleachie, the younger, Glengarry, Inverness-shire, in 1703. [NRS.CH1.2.5.2]

MACDONNELL, JOHN, probably from Inverness-shire, was captured at the Siege of Worcester on 2 September 1651, and transported via London aboard the <u>John and Sarah</u> to Boston, New England, in December 1651, landed there in February 1652. [Suffolk Deeds.1/5-6]

MACDONNELL, JOHN, a militiaman in Captain Burton's Company in Barbados in 1679. [H2.185]

MCDONELL, JOHN, son of Rorie McDonell of Glenaldaill, [Gleann Athadail], Morar, Inverness-shire, in 1703. [NRS.CH1.2.5.2]

MCDONELL, JOHN, in Essen, Moidart, Inverness-shire, in 1703. [NRS.CH1.2.5.2]

MCDONELL, JOHN, of Shian, [An Sithean], Glengarry, Inverness-shire, in 1703. [NRS.CH1.2.5.2]

MCDONELL, JOHN, of Ardnabie, Glengarry, Inverness-shire, in 1703. [NRS.CH1.2.5.2]

MCDONELL, JOHN, son of Ronald McDonell of Glengarry, Inverness-shire, in 1703. [NRS.CH1.2.5.2]

MCDONELL, JOHN, of Leek, Glengarry, Inverness-shire, in 1703. [NRS.CH1.2.5.2]

MCDONELL, JOHN, the younger of Wester Aberchalder, Glengarry, Inverness-shire, in 1703. [NRS.CH1.2.5.2]

MCDONELL, MARGARET, daughter of the late Donald McDonell of Scotus, brother of the laird of Glengarry, in Glen Elg, [Geann Eilg], and Knoydart, Inverness-shire, in 1703. [NRS.CH1.2.5.2]

MCDONELL, RANALD, brother of Allan McDonell, in Moidart, Inverness-shire, in 1703. [NRS.CH1.2.5.2]

MACDONELL, RANALD, of Culleachie, Glengarry, Inverness-shire, in 1703. [NRS.CH1.2.5.2]

MACDONELL, RANALD, in Pitmean, Glengarry, Inverness-shire, in 1703. [NRS.CH1.2.5.2]

MACDONELL, RANALD, of Glengarry, Inverness-shire, in 1703. [NRS.CH1.2.5.2]

MCDONELL, RANALD, of Kinloch Moidart, Inverness-shire, in 1703. [NRS.CH1.2.5.2]

MACDONELL, RANALD, of Barastill, Knoydart, Inverness-shire, in 1703. [NRS.CH1.2.5.2]

MACDONELL, RONALD, in Essen, Moidart, Inverness-shire, in 1703. [NRS.CH1.2.5.2]

MACDONELL, or MCALISTER, RONALD, in Glengarry, Inverness-shire, in 1703. [NRS.CH1.2.5.2]

MACDONELL, RORIE, in Moidart, Inverness-shire, in 1703. [NRS.CH1.2.5.2]

MACDONELL, RORIE, of Glenaldaill, Moidart, Inverness-shire, in 1703. [NRS.CH1.2.5.2]

MCEACHEN, DONALD, with two children in South Uist, in 1703. [NRS.CH1.2.5.2]

MCEACHEN, HECTOR, of Peinninreine, South Uist, in 1703. [NRS.CH1.2.5.2]

MCEACHEN, JOHN, in Kinnerres, testament, 30 August 1634, Comm. Inverness. [NRS]

MCEACHEN, JOHN, of Houbegg, South Uist, in 1703. [NRS.CH1.2.5.2]

MCEAN, ALASTER OIG, took goods from a ship of Leith at Barra, [Barraigh], bound from Glasgow to Danzig, a discharge was granted by Walter Stirling, a merchant of Glasgow to Danzig, a discharge was granted by Walter Stirling, a merchant burgess in Glasgow on 6 December 1627. [NRS.GD201.1.18]

MCEAN, ALEXANDER, a glazier [?] in Inverness on 25 October 1667. [IMB.233]

MCEAN, DONALD, in Mauld, Kilterlity, testament, 29 June 1633, Comm. Inverness. [NRS]

MCEAN GREASICH, DONALD, in Urray, [Urrach], or Kilchrist, Ross-shire, participated in the rebellion under James Graham, Marquis of Montrose, in 1649. [SHS.24.159]

MCEAN, VIC KERIE, DONALD, and his family, in Kirkton of Comar, Kiltarlity, Inverness-shire, in 1710. [NRS.CH1.2.5.2]

MCEAN, VIC QUEEN, DONALD, and his family, in Guisachan, Kiltarlity, Inverness-shire, in 1710. [NRS.CH1.2.5.2]

MCEAN, EVAN, in Stroan, Urquhart, testament, 1 September 1677, Comm. Inverness. [NRS]

MCEAN, HUTCHEON, a miller in Guisachen, Kiltarlity, Inverness-shire, in 1679. [IR.XXIV.82]

MCEAN, VIC JAMES, THOMAS, a witness in an inquest in Inverness on 23 March 1686. [IMB.343]

MCEAN, VIC COY, JOHN, and his family, in Guisachan, Kiltarlity, Inverness-shire, in 1710. [NRS.CH1.2.5.2]

MCEAN, WILLIAM, a 'mullich' in Inverness on 25 October 1667. [IMB.233]

MCEAN, VIC ANGUS, WILLIAM, and his family, in Guisachan, Kiltarlity, Inverness-shire, in 1710. [NRS.CH1.2.5.2]

MCEANVAYN, DUNCAN, in Inverness on 25 October 1667. [IMB.233]

MCEWAN, DONALD, in Errogy, Dores, [Dubhras], Inverness-shire, testament, 20 May 1631, Comm. Inverness. [NRS]

MCEWAN, FINLAY, in Standing Stanes, Inverness, testament, 30 October 1630, Comm. Inverness. [NRS]

MCEWAN, JOHN, in Inverness on 25 October 1667. [IMB.233]

MCFARQUHAR, ANGUS, in Aviemore, testament, 19 March 1678, Comm. Inverness. [NRS]

MCFARQUHAR, DONALD, in Domesdale Street, Inverness, a debtor for the stent in 1647. [IMB.194]

MCFARQUHAR, DUNCAN, in Urray or Kilchrist, Ross-shire, participated in the rebellion under James Graham, Marquis of Montrose, in 1649. [SHS.24.159]

MCFARQUHAR, JOHN, in Innerie, Rothiemurchus, [Rata Mhurchais], Inverness, testament, 27 November 1630, Comm. Inverness. [NRS]

MCFINLAY, CHRISTIAN, daughter of Donald McFinlay in Ardrannich, Conveth, testament, 19 June 1632, Comm. Inverness. [NRS]

MCFINLAY, CHRISTOPHER, and his family, in Kirkton of Comar, Kiltarlity, Inverness-shire, in 1710. [NRS.CH1.2.5.2]

MCFINLAY DONALD, a tailor, in Urray or Kilchrist, Ross-shire, participated in the rebellion under James Graham, Marquis of Montrose, in 1649. [SHS.24.159]

MCFINLAY GOWNE, JOHN BUY, in Urray, [Urrath], Ross-shire, or Kilchrist, [Cille Chriosd], Ross-shire, participated in the rebellion under James Graham, Marquis of Montrose, in 1649. [SHS.24.159]

MCFINDLEY, KENNETH, a chapman [pedlar] in Redcastle, [An Caisteal Ruadh], Ross-shire, imprisoned in Inverness Tolbooth, subject to bail of 300 merks Scots, on 22 April 1654. [IMB.209]

MCFINLAY, PAULL, in Strath Wasie, testament, 16 November 1632, Comm. Inverness. [NRS]

MCFRENSH, WILLIAM, miller at the King's Milne, [Mill], of Inverness, testament, 14 January 1669, Comm. Inverness. [NRS]

MCFRENCH, WILLIAM, in Inverness, was fined twenty pounds and withdrawal of burgess rights for fraud, on 28 June 1675. [IMB.263]

MCGALMISH, DONALD, a weaver in Inverness, testament, 30 March 1680, Comm. Inverness. [NRS]

MCGIBBON, FINDLAY, failed to appear before the High Burgh Court of Inverness on 10 January 1603. [ICB.3]

MCGILLANDRES, WILLIAM, in Rothiemurchus, Abernethy, testament, 5 May 1631, Comm. Inverness. [NRS]

MCGILANDRICE, WILLIAM, a smith in Connage, [A'Choinnis], Inverness-shire, in 1682. [SHS.24.114]

MCGILLICHALLUM, NIEL, in Duchamis, Arisaig, Inverness-shire, in 1703. [NRS.CH1.2.5.2]

MACGILLICHOAN, DONALD, a burgess of Dingwall, Ross-shire, a charter of lands in Dingwall dated 7 April 1621. [NRS.GD93.171]; with the consent of Grizel Fraser his wife, and Isobel Kemp his mother, and James Fraser of ….., to Hector McKenzie in Stroome, of lands in Dingwall, witnesses were John Fraser of Fairbairn, Murdoch McKenzie of Tollie, Roderick McKenzie of Knocbaxter, Ronald McKenzie of Culbo, John McKenzie in Dingwall, Roderick Dingwall, John Bard, William Dingwall, Hector McKenzie, Ronald Dingwall, John Kempt, all burgesses of Dingwall, Alexander Gray, Donald McChonchie voir, officers, and Roderick Urquhart a notary public. [SRS. Munro of Foulis Writs]

MCGILLIES, DONALD, in Romasalk, Glengarry, Inverness-shire, in 1703. [NRS.CH1.2.5.2]

MCGILLIES, or MCCOIL, NIEL, in Morar, Inverness-shire, in 1703. [NRS.CH1.2.5.2]

MCGILLIES, WILLIAM, in Kinloch Morar, Inverness-shire, in 1703. [NRS.CH1.2.5.2]

MCGILIGINE, JOHN, from Ross-shire, a student at King's College, Aberdeen, in 1670-1674. [KCA]

MCGILESON, DONALD, 'beyond the water', in Inverness on 25 October 1667. [IMB.233]

MCGILLISPICK, THOMAS, and his family, in Kiltarlity, Inverness-shire, in 1710. [NRS.CH1.2.5.2]

MCGILLIVRAY, ALEXANDER, in Dunmaglass, testament, 7 July 1677, Comm. Inverness. [NRS]

MCGILLIVRAY, BAYN, in Dunmaglass, [Dun Mac Glais], Inverness-shire, gave a bond of twenty merks Scots towards the construction of the bridge at Inverness, on 10 July 1682. [IMB.305]

MCGILLIVRAY, FARQUHAR, of Dunmaglass, [Dun Mac Glais], Inverness-shire, gave a bond of one hundred merks Scots towards the construction of the bridge at Inverness, on 10 July 1682. [IMB.305]

MCGILLIVRAY, JOHN, in Aberarder, Dunlichty, [Dun Fhlicheadaidh], testament, 19 November 1659, Comm. Inverness. [NRS]

MCGILLIVRAY, MAIRTAIN, of Overchalador, a tack, [lease], dated 9 November 1674. [NRS.RD4.36.94]

MCGILLIVRAY, WILLIAM, in Larges, Inverness-shire, gave a bond of twenty pounds Scots towards the construction of the bridge at Inverness, on 10 July 1682. [IMB.305]

MCGOWAN, ALEXANDER, in Inverness on 25 October 1667. [IMB.233]

MCGREGOR, PATRICK, in the Dell of Abernethy, testament, 31 July 1679, Comm. Inverness. [NRS]

MCHAMAS, DONALD, in Inverness on 25 October 1667. [IMB.233]

MCHATICH, ALEXANDER, a seaman in Inverness, testament in 1633, Comm. Inverness. [NRS]

MCHENDRICK, FINDLAY, in Bunchruben, Dores, testament, 12 June 1630, Comm. Inverness. [NRS]

MCHUTCHEON, ALEXANDER, in Inverness on 25 October 1667. [IMB.233]

MCHUTCHEON, ALEXANDER, a smith in Guisachan, Kiltarlity, Inverness-shire in 1679. [IR.XXIV.82]

MCHUTCHEON, DUNCAN, in Comar, Kiltarlity, Inverness-shire in 1679. [IR.XXIV.82]

MCHUTCHEON, WILLIAM, a 'wentner', [chimney sweep?], in Inverness on 25 October 1667. [IMB.233]

MCHUTCHEON, THOMAS MOR, in Kilmorack, Inverness-shire in 1673. [IR.XXIV.80]

MCHUTCHEON, WILLIAM, in Comar, Kiltarlity, Inverness-shire in 1679. [IR.XXIV.82]

MCINNES, FARQUHAR, in Glenbeg, [An Gleann Beg], testament, 27 October 1669, Comm. Inverness. [NRS]

MCINNES, JOHN, in Tulloch, [An Tulach], Urquhart, testament, 10 June 1634, Comm. Inverness. [NRS]

MCINNES, ..., a soldier in Captain Allemby's Company of Militia in Barbados, on 6 January 1679. [H2/155]

MCINTAGGART, FARQUHAR, in Fanellan, testament, 17 June 1667, Comm. Inverness. [NRS]

MCINTEER, JOHN, in Knockie, Abertarff, [Obar Thairbh], testament, 16 June 1632, Comm. Inverness. [NRS]

MCINTOSH, AENEAS, from Inverness, a student at King's College, Aberdeen, in 1677. [KCA]

MCINTOSH, ALESTAIR, was buried in St Peter's parish, Barbados, in 1679. [H2.89]

MACINTOSH, ALEXANDER, from Ross-shire. a student at King's College, Aberdeen, in 1659. [KCA]

MACKINTOSH, ALEXANDER, of Far, Inverness-shire, gave a bond of fifty merks towards the construction of the bridge at Inverness, on 10 July 1682. [IMB.305]

MCINTOSH, ALEXANDER, in Culchlochrie, was subjected to a precept of poinding for payment of a bond due to James MacIntosh a merchant in Inverness, on 31 July 1690. [NRS.GD23.10.302]

MCINTOSH, ANGUS, son of Lauchlan McIntosh of Borlum, was apprenticed to William Milne a merchant in Edinburgh on 16 April 1662. [REA]

MCINTOSH, ANGUS, in Coull, testament, 16 July 1667 Comm. Inverness. [NRS]

MCINTOSH, ANGUS, of Holme, [An Tuilm], Inverness-shire, eldest son of the deceased William Mcintosh of Holme, a burgess of Inverness, was admitted as a burgess and guildsbrother of Inverness on 27 September 1686. [IMB.345]; may have pastured his herd at the Rogg's end of Holme which strayed onto the lands of Inverness, a court case on 21 June 1680. [IMB.286]

MCINTOSH, ANGUS, spouse of Donald Fraser in Little Garth, testament 13 February 1678 Comm. Inverness. [NRS]

MCINTOSH, DONALD, minister at Farr from 1674, later at Duthil, [Daothal], Inverness-shire, in 1695. [F.VII.106]

MCINTOSH, DUNCAN, son of Alexander McIntosh in Inverness was apprenticed to Hector McKenzie a merchant in Edinburgh on 3 June 1674. [REA]

MCINTOSH, HELEN, relict of Patrick Gordon in Raitt, [Rata], testament, 7 September 1666 Comm. Inverness. [NRS]

MCINTOSH, HENRY, purchased a plantation in Surinam in November 1674, a petition dated 8 June 1676, a planter in Surinam, probate 21 January 1679, Barbados. [Cal.SPCol.1575.683]

MCINTOSH, JAMES, a stent [tax] collector in Inverness on 19 April 1672. [IMB.252]; a merchant of Inverness, on 9 April 1679. [NRS.AC7.5]; took the Test Oath on 19 December 1681. [IMB.299]; raised a Precept of Poimding for payment of bonds on 31 July 1690, against [1] Alexander Fraser McSime Anderson in Inches; Donald McColl oig alias Mcbean in Balloan; Alexander McIntosh in Culchlachrie; Alexander Ross in Ballynabely of Drakies; John Roy Dallas in Wester Urquahall. [NRS.GD23.10.302]

MCINTOSH, JOHN, a merchant in Inverness, a charter party, dated 30 September 1674. [NRS.RD2.38.73]

MCINTOSH, JOHN, in Flemington, Petty, testament, 1 October 1677 Comm. Inverness. [NRS]

MCINTOSH, JOHN, the elder, under an act of Inverness Town Council of 18 October 1680, was required to supply the town guard with coal and candles every night. [IMB.297]

MCINTOSH, JOHN, in Ellarick, gave a bond of forty pounds Scots towards the construction of the bridge at Inverness, on 10 July 1682. [IMB.305]

MCINTOSH, JOHN, of Dalmigavie, [Dail Mhigeachaidh], Inverness-shire, gave a bond of forty pounds Scots towards the construction of the bridge at Inverness, on 10 July 1682. [IMB.305]

MCINTOSH, JOHN, the younger, was appointed as Lieutenant of a Militia Company, to protect Inverness from McDonald of Keppoch and his rebels, 3 September 1688. [IMB.7]

MCINTOSH, LACHLAN, of Kellachie, testament, 18 September 1634 Comm. Inverness. [NRS]

MCINTOSH, LACHLAN, of Stroan, gave a bond of fifty merks Scots towards the construction of the bridge at Inverness, on 10 July 1682. [IMB.305]

MACKINTOSH, LAUCHLAN, of Aberarder, [Obar Ardair], Inverness-shire, gave a bond of one hundred pounds Scots towards the construction of the bridge at Inverness, on 10 July 1682. [IMB.305]

MACKINTOSH, LAUCHLAN, of Kinrara, gave a bond of one hundred pounds Scots towards the construction of the bridge at Inverness, on 10 July 1682. [IMB.305]

MCINTOSH, ROBERT, of Beacher, gave a bond of twenty pounds Scots towards the construction of the bridge at Inverness, on 10 July 1682. [IMB.305]

MCINTOSH, WILLIAM, of Borlum, testament, 15 August 1631 Comm. Inverness. [NRS]

MCINTOSH, WILLIAM, of Torcastle, [Torr a'Chaisteil], Inverness-shire, versus Allan Cameron of Lochiel, papers from 1655 until 1659. [NRS.GD176.443]

MCINTOSH, WILLIAM, son of Daniel McIntosh of Kellochie, was apprenticed to Duncan McIntosh a merchant in Edinburgh on 4 July 1677. [REA]

MCINTOSH, WILLIAM, of Conadge, [A'Choinnis], Inverness-shire, was imprisoned in Inverness Tolbooth due to a debt of three hundred and forty pounds, also two thousand merks owing the Sir George McKenzie of Rosehaugh. John Forrester and David Denoon, subscribed to a bond of one thousand merks payable should William McIntosh escaped from prison, on 13 November 1682. [IMB.312]

MCINTOSH, WILLIAM, was appointed as Captain of a Militia Company, to protect Inverness from McDonald of Keppoch and his rebels, 3 September 1688. [IMB.7]

MCINTOSH, WILLIAM, of Borlum, [Borlum], Inverness-shire, gave a bond of one hundred pounds Scots towards the construction of the bridge at Inverness, on 10 July 1682. [IMB.305]; granted a tack [lease] to his son Joseph McIntosh on 30 October 1697. [NRS.GD214.338]

MCIVOR, DONALD, in Kilmorack, Inverness-shire, in 1673. [IR.XXIV.80]

MCIVOR, DONALD, in Erchless, [Earghlais], Kiltarlity, Inverness-shire, in 1679. [IR.XXIV.82]

MCIVOR, DONALD, in Mauld, [Mald], Kiltarlity, Inverness-shire, in 1673. [IR.XXIV.82]

MCIVER, WILLIAM, a miller at Culcabock, [Cuil na Cabaig], testament, 27 January 1679, Comm. Inverness. [NRS]

MCJAMES, JOHN, in Farlattie, Kingussie, [Ceann a'Ghiuthsaich], testament, 15 November 1633, Comm. Inverness. [NRS]

MCJAMES, WILLIAM, a tailor in Inverness, was ordered to pay William McRichie there the sum of 16 shillings due for two ells of grey cloth, on 3 December 1602. [IBC.3]

MCJOCK, JOHN ROY, in Urray or Kilchrist, Ross-shire, participated in the rebellion under James Graham, Marquis of Montrose, in 1649. [SHS.24.159]

MACKAY, [MACAOIDH], AENEAS, Major of Livingstone's Regiment of Dragoons at the Battle of Cromdale in Strathspey on 1 May 1690. [BK.177]

MACKAY, AENEAS, son of Lord Reay and his wife Barbara Mackay of Scourie, [Sgobharaidh], Sutherland, an officer of the Scots Brigade in Dutch Service, married Margaret von Puckler in 1692, he died in 1697. [SP.VII.171]; founder of the Dutch branch of Clan Mackay. [BM]

MCKAY, ALEXANDER, was appointed as Lieutenant of a Militia Company, to protect Inverness from McDonald of Keppoch and his rebels, 3 September 1688. [IMB.7]

MACKAY, ANGUS, of Melness, [Taobh Mhealainis], Sutherland, granted lands in Kintail, Wester Ross, to his brother John Mackay,

Lord Reay, in exchange for a bond of 2000 merks, certain lands were, brother of Sir James wadset [mortgaged] to the late William McAllan, his foster father, and his wife Margaret Gordon with liferent to her, deed dated in Durness, Sutherland, on 27 January 1666. Witnesses were Thomas Manson, the Sheriff Clerk of Sutherland, Thomas Manson his servant, and Andrew Manson, a writer [lawyer] in Dornoch, Easter Ross. [NRS.GD84.1.27.2]

MACKAY, ANGUS, bailie of Lochinver, [Loch an Inbhir], in Assynt, Wester Ross, a bond dated 23 April 1674. [NRS.RD2.37.332]

MACKAY, ANGUS, possibly from Sutherland, a Captain of Mackay's Regiment at the Battle of Killiecrankie in Perthshire, was killed on 27 July 1689. [BK.96/207]

MACKAY, ANNA, sister of Lord Reay, spouse of Alexander McDonald, brother of Sir James McDonald of Sleat baronet. A marriage contract dated 12 March 1674. [NRS.RD2.37.106]

MACKAY, DANIEL, married [1] Honora Gulley on 17 November 1659, and [2] Christina ... on 15 April 1661, both times in Christchurch, Barbados. [PR]

MACKAY, DONALD, in Fingask, Wardlaw, testament, 1 December 1631, Comm. Inverness. [NRS]

MACKAY, Sir DONALD, Lord Reay, born 1590, from Sutherland, on 3 March 1626 was empowered to raise a regiment of 2000 men for service on the continent, sailed from Cromarty on 6 October 1626, Colonel of Mackay's Regiment in Danish Service in 1626, and in Swedish Service in 1629. [TGSI.VIII.1228]; in Amsterdam, the Netherlands on 23 December 1629. He sailed from Thurso, Caithness, to Denmark in 1648 and died in Copenhagen in 1649. The King of Denmark shipped his body to the Kyle of Tongue, [Tunga], Sutherland, which was buried in the church at Kirkiboll, [Circ Abol], Sutherland. [NRS.GD84.2.177][TGSI.8.129][BM]; a bond due to John McKay, a merchant burgess of Thurso for £600 dated 3 March 1636, witnesses were Alexander Munro minister at Durness, Sutherland], William Aitchison, Patrick Murdo, and John McLeod servants to Lord Reay. [NRS.GD84.1.3.3];a bond for 1000 merks due to Paul McKay in Durness, [Diuirnis],Sutherland, dated on 4 September whom failing to his daughter Jean Innes and his wife Elizabeth Ballenden, dated 30 October 1637. [NRS.GD84.1.3.3]; as

His Majesty's Governor of the Northern Shires, Donald Mackay, Lord Reay, issued a Commission of Fire and Sword to John Mackay master of Reay, Colonel of the Strathnavar Regiment, to join with other forces of Caithness and Sutherland to defend the borders of Sutherland dated 21 May 1646. [NRS.GD84.2.203]

MACKAY, DONALD, a lawyer in Edinburgh, son of Captain William Mackay of Borley, raised a company of men for the Darien Expedition, from Leith on 17 July 1698 bound for the Isthmus of Darien in Panama, landed there on 28 September 1698, he returned to Britain in August 1699 for an audience with King William, then from London to Edinburgh on 28 August 1699. On 21 September 1699 he was bound for Darien aboard the Rising Sun by way of Montserrat, St Kitts, and Port Royal, Jamaica, but was drowned attempting to harpoon a shark. [BM.174 quoting the Blackcastle manuscript]

MACKAY, DONALD, with a company of men from Strathnavar, [Srath Nabhair], Sutherland, died on the voyage bound for Darien, Panama, in 1699. [BM.174]

MACKAY, DONALD, a merchant in Inverness, a debtor of James Gordon, a merchant in Edinburgh, in 1707. [NRS.AC9.12.62]

MACKAY, HUGH, an officer of Mackay's Regiment in Danish Service in 1626, and in Swedish Service in 1629. [TGSI.8.188]

MACKAY, HEW, third son of Lord Donald Mackay and Barbara McKenzie, died before 1642. [BM.142]

MACKAY, Major HUGH, in Keldall, an assignment in favour of his children, by his first wife Euphan Mackay, John, Hugh, Anna, and Christian, dated at Durness, Sutherland, on 3 February 1665, witnesses were Thomas Manson a Notary Public, Thomas Manson his servant, and Andrew Manson a writer [lawyer] in Dornoch, Sutherland. [NRS.GD84.1.21.3B]

MACKAY, HUGH, of Scourie, [Sgobharaidh], Sutherland, a deed in 1685, [NRS.RD3.66.357]; Colonel of Mackay's Regiment in 1689; Major General Hugh Mackay ordered the laird of Balgowan, [Naile a'Ghobhainn], chief of the Clan Ross, to send one hundred of his best armed men to garrison Inverness, on 16 May 1689. [NRS.NRAS.276.2.22]

MACKAY, Captain HUGH, of Borlay, on St Kitts by 1700. [NRS.GD84.Sec.1.22.9b]

MCKAY, JAMES, a soldier who was given a pass to travel to the Netherlands, in 1610. [TNA.E157.16]

MACKAY, JAMES, in Raitts, [Rata], testament, 8 March 1678 Comm. Inverness. [NRS]

MACKAY, JAMES, Lieutenant Colonel of Mackay's Regiment, was killed at the Battle of Killiecrankie, Perthshire, in 1689.

MACKAY, JOHN, eldest son of Sir Donald Mackay of Strathnavar, [Srath Nabhair], Sutherland, was admitted as a burgess of Aberdeen on 18 September 1624. [ABR]

MACKAY, JOHN, probably from Sutherland, was captured at the Siege of Worcester in 1651, was transported via London aboard the John and Sarah to New England in November 1651. [Suffolk Deeds, 1-56] [NWI.I.153]

MACKAY, JOHN, Lord Reay, and Angus Mackay and spouse Katherine Gunn, a contract of wadset [mortgage] on 1 May 1658, later a sasine of the lands of Meiness in the barony of Kintail, Wester Ross, on 4 August 1676. [NRS.GD84.1.27.8]

MACKAY, JOHN, son of Lord Donald Mackay and his first wife Barbara McKenzie, became 2nd Lord Reay from 1649 until his death in 1680. As a Royalist he and his men attacked Inverness on 22 February 1650, the fought at the Battle of Balvenie, [Baile Bhainidh], Banffshire, where he was captured and imprisoned in Edinburgh until he escaped in 1650. [BM]

MACKAY, JOHN, sin of John Mackay in Golspie, Sutherland, was apprenticed to Patrick Steill a merchant in Edinburgh on6 June 1677. [REA]

MACKAY, JOHN, in Rothiemurchus, testament, 20 March 1678 Comm. Inverness. [NRS]

MACKAY, JOHN, a soldier of Captain John Burrow's Company of Militia on Barbados in 1679. [H2.182]

MACKAY, JOHN, a seaman aboard <u>HMS Chatham</u> probate 1698, Prerogative Court of Canterbury. [TNA]

MACKAY, MURDO, eldest son of Robert Mackay in Letterwall, a bond for 1000 merks dated 12 December 1664. [NRS.GD84.1.22.2B]

MACKAY, NEIL, son of Donald Mackay of Scourie, [Sgobharaidh], Sutherland, with the consent of his brother Hugh Mackay, resigned various lands in the Dioceses of Caithness and Regality of Sutherland to Sir Donald Mackay of Strathnavar on 19 April 1620. [NRS.GD84.1.11.4]

MACKAY, Sir PATRICK, of Largie, [An Learg], an officer of Mackay of Lairg's Regiment was wounded at the Pass of Oldenburg in Germany in 1627, died in Copenhagen, Denmark, in 1628. [BM.134][SAA.II.123]

MACKEY, PETER, a mariner aboard <u>HMS Norwich</u> probate 1699 Prerogative Court of Canterbury. [TNA]

MACKAY, ROBERT, a soldier of 1st Company of Cockburn's Regiment in Swedish Service in 1609. [SIS.217]

MACKAY, ROBERT, a merchant in Tain, Ross-shire, a bond dated3 September 1661. [NRS.RD3.2.632]

MACKAY, ROBERT, a Captain of Mackay's Regiment, was wounded at the Battle of Killiecrankie, Perthshire, in 1689.

MACKAY, RODERICK, from Strathnavar, Sutherland, a student at King's College, Aberdeen, in 1658-1660. [KCA]

MACKAY, WILLIAM, son of Donald Mackay of Scourie, [Sgobharaidh], Sutherland, a Captain of Mackay's Regiment in Danish Service in 1626, in Swedish Service in 1629, later a Lieutenant Colonel of the Swedish Army, was killed at the Battle of Lutzen, Saxony, on 6 November 1632. [TGSI.VIII.187][SAA.II.127]

MACKAY, WILLIAM, a Captain of Mackay's Regiment in Danish Service in 1626, and in Swedish Service in 1629. [TGSI.VIII.187]

MACKAY, WILLIAM, from Strathnavar, Sutherland, a student at King's College, Aberdeen, in 1658.-1660. [KCA]

MACKAY, WILLIAM, of Bighouse, [Biogas], Sutherland, a bond dated 25 June 1661. [NRS.RD2.1.335]

MACKAY, WILLIAM, of Golval, [Golbhal], Sutherland, minister at Rogart, [Sgire Raoghaird], Sutherland, from 1662 until 1668, then at Lairg, [Luirg], Sutherland, from 1668, husband of Margaret Sutherland. [F.7.92]

MACKAY, WILLIAM, son of Donald Mackay, 1st Lord Reay, a sasine of Kinloch in 1669, husband of Ann, daughter of Colonel Hugh Mackay of Scourie, Sutherland, parents of George Mackay. [BM.143]

MACKAY, ..., a Lieutenant of Mackay's Regiment in Danish Service in 1626, and in Swedish Service in 1629, later promoted in Ruthven's Regiment. [TGSI.VIII.187]

MCKENNETH, ALEXANDER, in Raitts, [Rata], Inverness, testament, 22 October 1680, Comm. Inverness. [NRS]

MCKENZIE, AGNES, ANNABELL, and ISOBEL, heirs and daughter of the late John McKenzie of Fairburn, were granted several properties in Inverness-shire, on 6 June 1655. [RGSS.X.406]

MCKENZIE, [MACCOINNICH], ALEXANDER, Chamberlain of Lewis, [Leodhas], in the Outer Hebrides, on 11 April 1628. [NRS.AC7.2.62]

MCKENZIE, ALEXANDER, brother of Sir John McKenzie of Tarbat, [Tairbeart], Ross-shire, was admitted as a burgess and guilds-brother of Aberdeen on 4 April 1637. [ABR]

MCKENZIE, ALEXANDER, second son of the deceased John McKenzie of Gairloch, a marriage contract with Katherine McKenzie, daughter of John McKenzie of Gairloch, [Gearloch], Wester Ross, dated 18 February 1640. [NRS.NRAS.143.bundle 30]

MCKENZIE, ALEXANDER, the younger, of Coull, [A'Chuil], Ross-shire, a student at King's College, Aberdeen, in 1652. [KCA; was admitted as a burgess and guilds-brother of Aberdeen on 22 January 1663. [ABR]

MCKENZIE, ALEXANDER, of Gairloch, Wester Ross, a marriage contract with Barbara McKenzie, daughter of Sir George McKenzie of Tarbert, [An Tairbeart], Ross-shire, dated 4 March 1670. [NRS.NRAS.143.Bundle 30]

MCKENZIE, ALEXANDER, of Kilcoy, [Cuil Challaidh], Ross-shire, was released from Inverness Tolbooth on 28 May 1683. [IMB.316]

MCKENZIE, ALEXANDER, of Applecross, [Abar Crosain], Ross-shire, a student at King's College, Aberdeen, in 1667. [KCA]

MCKENZIE, ALEXANDER, of Ballone, a marriage contract with Lillias McKenzie, sister of Alexander McKenzie of Gairloch, Wester Ross, dated 9 February 1670. [NRS.NRAS.143.bundle 30]

MCKENZIE, ALEXANDER, of Ardloch, a marriage contract with Barbara McKenzie, relict of Hugh Fraser of Kinnaries, dated 4 March 1670. [NRS.NRAS.143.bundle 30]

MCKENZIE, ALEXANDER, of Applecross, [Abar Crosain]. Wester Ross, versus the Countess of Wemyss, in 1684. [NRS.CS230.MC1/6]

MCKENZIE, ALEXANDER, of Gairloch, [Gearrloch], Ross-shire, a deed in 1685. [NRS.RD4.

MCKENZIE, ALEXANDER, son of the Earl of Seaforth, a student at Douai in 1685. [RSC.57]

MCKENZIE, ALEXANDER, born 1681, was transported to Pennsylvania, indentured in Chester County, Pa., on 5 August 1697. [SG.29.1.13]

MCKENZIE, ANGUS from Ross-shire, a student at King's College, Aberdeen, in 1646. [KCA]

MCKENZIE, BERNARD, born 1657, son of Captain Daniel McKenzie and his wife Nance Dunbar, was educated at King's College, Aberdeen, a schoolmaster in Fortrose, Easter Ross, then minister at Cromarty from 1678 until deprived as an Episcopalian in 1690, he died on 30 July 1713 and was buried in Fortrose. [F.VII.5]; a deed in 1685. [NRS.RD4.55.804]

MCKENZIE, CALUM {?}, from Ross-shire, a student at King's College, Aberdeen, in 1667. [KCA]

MCKENZIE, CHARLES, brother of the laird of Redcastle, [An Caisteal Dearg], Ross-shire, a student at King's College, Aberdeen, in 1668. [KCA]

MCKENZIE, COLIN, of Redcastle, Ross-shire, a student at King's College, Aberdeen, in 1648. [KCA]; of Redcastle, a contract dated 11 August 1674. [NRS.RD3.37.66]

MCKENZIE, Mr COLIN, of Kinnock, Urray, [Urrath], Ross-shire, admitted being a participant in the Royalist uprising led by James Graham, Marquis of Montrose, into England and at the Siege of Inverness in 1649. [SHS.14.158] [NRS.CH2.921]

MCKENZIE, COLIN, brother german of John McKenzie of Applecross, [A'Chomriach], and Margaret McKenzie, eldest daughter of Murdo McKenzie of Sand, a marriage contract subscribed at Dingwall on 20 November 1657. Witnesses were Hector MacKenzie of Assynt, Alexander MacKenzie of Pitglassie, Alexander MacKenzie, brother german to the laird of Gairloch, John MacKenzie in Aijne Mill, and Mr Donald Bayne writer of the deed. [TGSI.14.52] [NRS.NRAS.143.bundle 30]

MCKENZIE, COLIN, servant to the Earl of Seaforth, was admitted as a burgess of Aberdeen on 22 January 1663. [ABR]

MCKENZIE, COLIN, of Balmuchy, Collector of Supply for Ross-shire, a deed dated 1695. [NRS.RD4.77.754]

MCKENZIE, DANIEL, of Loggie, [An Lagaidh], Ross-shire, versus ....McLeod and the excise of Lewis, 5/19 November 1666. [IMB.231]

MCKENZIE, DUNCAN, from Ross-shire, a student at King's College, Aberdeen, in 1677. [KCA]

MCKENZIE, GEORGE, muster master of Thomas McKenzie's Company in Denmark in 1628. [SAA.II.124]

MCKENZIE, GEORGE, of Kildyn, [Cill Duinn], Ross-shire, was admitted as a burgess of Aberdeen on 19 September 1628. [ABR]

MCKENZIE, GEORGE, of Tarbart, [An Tairbeart], Ross-shire, a student at King's College, Aberdeen, in 1647. [KCA]

MCKENZIE, GEORGE, from Ross-shire, a student at King's College, Aberdeen, in 1650. [KCA]

MCKENZIE, GEORGE, of Kildun, [Cill Duinn], Ross-shire, tacksman of Aignish, [Aiginis], in Lewis, Outer Hebrides, in 1680s, and son Colin. [IR.XXIV.100]

MCKENZIE, Captain GEORGE, in New York on 15 August 1689. [NYD.3.614] [SPAWI.1689.352/360]

MCKENZIE, GEORGE, sub-tacksman of Excise in Inverness, Ross & Cromarty, Sutherland, and Caithness, a petition dated 1697. [NRS.E80.17]

MCKENZIE, HECTOR, of Farburn, Urray or Kilchrist, Ross-shire, participated in the rebellion under James Graham, Marquis of Montrose, in 1649. [SHS.24.159]

MCKENZIE, HECTOR, from Ross-shire, a student at King's College, Aberdeen, in 1660. [KCA]

MCKENZIE, HECTOR, son of Rorie McKenzie of Davochmalouch, was apprenticed to William Milne a merchant in Edinburgh on 15 November 1665. [REA]

MCKENZIE, HECTOR, of Assynt, [Asainn], Wester Ross, a bond dated 6 January 1674. [NRS.RD2.36.531]

MCKENZIE, HUGH, a mariner aboard HMS Chatham probate 1698 Prerogative Court of Canterbury. [TNA]

MCKENZIE, ISOBEL, ANNABEL, and AGNES, daughters and heirs portioners of John McKenzie of Fairburn, were granted lands, property, castles, fishing rights, and others in Inverness-shire, which had pertained to Hew Fraser, Master of Lovat, now Lord Lovat, on 6 June 1655. [RGSS.X.406]

MCKENZIE, JAMES, from Ross-shire, a student at King's College, Aberdeen, in 1667. [KCA]

MCKENZIE, JAMES, son of James, Viscount of Tarbet, was admitted as a burgess and guilds-brother of Edinburgh on 30 August 1699. [REB]

MCKENZIE, JAMES, a merchant in Inverness, a deed in 1694. [NRS.RD4.75.683]

MCKENZIE, JOHN, of Fairburn, was granted a charter of Monar on 20 April 1620. [NRS.GD46.18.15]

MCKENZIE, JOHN, of Coul, [Cuil], Ross-shire, was permitted to build a sepulchre in Chancery on 30 October 1635. Witnesses were John, Bishop of Ross, Chancery on 30 October 1635. Witnesses were John, Bishop of Ross, Patrick Durham, Dean of Ross, James Ainslie, precentor, John Munro, Chancellor, Gilbert Murray, subdeacon, R. Munro in Rosskeen, David Munro, in Killearnan, John Malcolm subdeacon of Ross, Thomas Young, rector of Kilmichael, David Ross, rector of Logie Easter, Murdoch McKenzie, rector of Dingwall, and Alexander Hossack, rector of Kilmuimesr, Tongue, dated 30 October 1635. [NRS.GD1.1149.7]

MCKENZIE, JOHN, MA, minister at Urray and Tarradale, [Tarradel], Ross-shire, from 1636 until 1639 when he was deposed for opposing the Covenant. [F.7.49]

MCKENZIE, JOHN, from Ross-shire, a student at King's College, Aberdeen, in 1647. [KCA]

MCKENZIE, JOHN, of Davochcairn, Alness, [Alanais], Ross-shire, admitted participating in the Royalist uprising led by James Graham, Marquis of Montrose, and at the Siege of Inverness in 1649. [SHS.24.157/158][NRS.CH2.92.1]

MCKENZIE, JOHN, of Applecross, [A'Chomraich], Wester Ross, in Urray or Kilchrist, participated in the Royalist uprising led by James Graham, Marquis of Montrose, in 1649. [SHS.24.171]

MCKENZIE, JOHN, son of the laird of Coull, Ross-shire, a student at King's College, Aberdeen, in 1668. [KCA]

MCKENZIE, JOHN, from Ardlair, Ross-shire, a student at King's College, Aberdeen, in 1676. [KCA]

MCKENZIE, JOHN, an indentured servant of John Laing in Middlesex County, New Jersey, was granted land there on 17 January 1693. [NJSA.EJ Deeds, Liber D]

MCKENZIE, KATHERINE, spouse of Alexander Fraser of Riligg, testament, 12 November 1679, Comm. Inverness. [NRS]

MCKENZIE, KENNETH, a servant in Urray or Kilchrist, Ross-shire, participated in the rebellion under James Graham, Marquis of Montrose, in 1649. [SHS.24.159]

MCKENZIE, KENNETH, of Gairloch, [Gearrloch], Wester Ross, participated in the rebellion under James Graham, Marquis of Montrose, in 1649. [SHS.24.171]; was granted lands in Inverness-shire formerly possessed by Isobel McKenzie, on 19 June 1658. [RGSS.X.654]

MCKENZIE, JOHN, son of Mr George McKenzie of Kildin, was apprenticed to John Jollie a merchant burgess of Edinburgh on 24 October 1694. [REA]

MCKENZIE, KENNETH, of Assynt, [Asaint], Sutherland participated in the rebellion under James Graham, Marquis of Montrose, in 1649. [SHS.24.159]

MCKENZIE, KENNETH, a property owner in Dingwall, Easter Ross, a reference in 1652. [RGSS.X.16]

MCKENZIE, KENNETH, of Gairloch, Wester Ross, a marriage contract with Janet Cuthbert, second daughter of John Cuthbert of Castlehill, Inverness, dated 17 December 1658. [NRS.NRAS.143.bundle 30]

MCKENZIE, KENNETH, of Suddie, [Suidhe], Ross-shire, was admitted a burgess and guilds-brother of Aberdeen on 22 January 1663. [ABR]

MCKENZIE, KENNETH, of Assynt, Sutherland, a student at King's College, Aberdeen, in 1667. [KCA]

MCKENZIE, Sir KENNETH, of Coul, Contin, [Cunndainn], Ross-shire, was created as a baronet on 16 October 1673. [NRS.GD1.1149]

MCKENZIE, KENNETH, eldest son of the Earl of Seaforth, was admitted as a burgess and guilds-brother of Aberdeen on 10 February 1675. [ABR]

MCKENZIE, KENNETH, of Kildin, [Cuill Duinn], Ross-shire, the younger, a student at King's College, Aberdeen, in 1677. [KCA]

MCKENZIE, KENNETH, of Glen Marqueis, a deed in 1685. [NRS.RD4.57.762]

MCKENZIE, Mr KENNETH, son of Viscount Tarbet, was admitted as a burgess and guilds-brother of Edinburgh on 16 March 1687. [REB]

MCKENZIE, KENNETH, of Ranitries, graduated MA from King's College, Aberdeen, minister at Fearn from 1689 until deposed in 1691, husband of Jean McKenzie. [F.VII.56]

MCKENZIE, KENNETH, of Gairloch, a marriage contract with Margaret McKenzie, youngest daughter of the deceased Sir Roy McKenzie of Findon, dated 21 April 1696. [NRS.NRAS.143.Bundle 30]

MCKENZIE, Mr KENNETH, of Cromarty, in 1704. [NRS.AC9.82]

MCKENZIE, MARGARET, spouse of Patrick Grant in Carnoch, [A'Charnach] Ross-shire, testament, 19 May 1666, Comm. Inverness. [NRS]

MCKENZIE, MURDOCH, graduated MA from Marischal College in Aberdeen in 1622, chaplain of Mackay's Regiment in Danish Service in 1626 and in Swedish Service in 1629 under King Gustavus Adolphus of Sweden, chaplain of Mackay's Regiment in Danish Service 1626 later minister in Suddie, [Suidhe], Ross-shire. [TGSI.VIII.189 F.7.17][SAA.II.119]; a minister in Inverness on 31 March 1641. [IMB.178]; minister in Ross-shire, Inverness and Elgin, Episcopal Bishop of Moray from 1662 to 1677, then Bishop of Orkney from 1677 until his death in February 1688. [Keith.228]

MCKENZIE, MURDOCH, of Farburn, a student at King's College, Aberdeen, in 1667. [KCA]

MCKENZIE, MURDO, son of John McKenzie a servant of Colin, Lord Kintail, was apprenticed to Alexander McCulloch a wright in Edinburgh, on 16 July 1623. [REA]

MCKENZIE, MURDO, born 1606, a soldier 99 was given a pass to travel to Amsterdam, Holland, in 1631. [TNA.E157.15]

MCKENZIE, Mr MURDO, a property owner in Dingwall, Easter Ross, a reference in 1652. [RGSS.X.16][TGSI.VIII.189][F.7.17]

MCKENZIE, NORMAN, an indentured servant brought to New Jersey by Captain Thomas Pearson of the Thomas and Benjamin on 5 November 1684 was sold to Mr David Mudie. [NJSA.EJ Deeds Liber A.184]

MCKENZIE, RODERICK, graduated MA from King's College, Aberdeen, in 1649, minister at Avoch, [Abhach], Ross-shire, from 1668 to 1669. [F.VII.2]

MCKENZIE, RODERICK, of Avoch, [Abhach], Ross-shire, son of John McKenzie archdeacon of Ross and minister at Fodderty, [Fodhraitidh], Episcopalian minister at Avoch from 1668 until his death on 7 March 1710. [F.VII.2]

MCKENZIE, RODERICK, a writer [lawyer] in Edinburgh, son of Alexander McKenzie of Culcovie, was granted several lands and properties in Ross-shire and Inverness-shire on 13 July 1655. which formerly pertained to the Earl of Seaforth. [RGSS.X.440]

MCKENZIE, RODERICK, a burgess of Inverness, was admitted as a burgess and guilds-brother of Aberdeen on 22 January 1663. [ABR]

MCKENZIE, RODERICK, of Redcastle, a student at King's College, Aberdeen, in 1668. [KCA]

MCKENZIE, RODERICK, of Applecross, a student at King's College, Aberdeen, in 1667. [KCA]

MCKENZIE, RODERICK, of Davachmaluock, a bond dated 11 March 1674. [NRS.RD2.37.92]

MCKENZIE, RODERICK, of 'Kinquhillidram', brother of the Earl of Seaforth, was admitted as a burgess and guilds-brother of Aberdeen on 4 March 1675. [ABR]

MCKENZIE, RODERICK, from Ross-shire, a student at King's College, Aberdeen, in 1677. [KCA]

MCKENZIE, Mr RODERICK, son of Alexander McKenzie of Husibost, was apprenticed to William Borthwick, a surgeon in Edinburgh on 20 October 1680. [REA]

MCKENZIE, RORIE, of Davachmoluagg, Urray or Kilchrist, participated in the rebellion under James Graham, Marquis of Montrose, in 1649. [SHS.24.159/165]

MCKENZIE, RORIE, fiar of Fairburn, in Urray or Kilchrist, participated in the rebellion under James Graham, Marquis of Montrose, in 1649. [SHS.24.159/160]

MCKENZIE, RORIE, of Tollie, [Tollaidh], Ross-shire, whose lands were apprised in settlement of debt, in June 1652. [RGSS.X.16]

MCKENZIE, RORY, of Ardefaylie, deceased, late resident near Rosemarkie, [Ros Mhaircnidh], Easter Ross, in 1654. [RGSS.X.356]

MCKENZIE, RORY, of Alness, was appointed an advocate for Inverness to function in the Court of Session, on 13 October 1679, with an annual pension of 20 merks Scots. [IMB.281]

MCKENZIE, Sir RORY, of Findon, [Fionndun], requested that Alexander McKenzie of Culbowie, imprisoned in Inverness Tolbooth for debt be released if security be provided of debt due, on 19 August 1682. [IMB.308]

MCKENZIE, SIMON, from Ross-shire, a student at King's College, Aberdeen, in 1660. [KCA]

MCKENZIE, SIMON, son of Kenneth McKenzie of Coull, was admitted as a burgess and guilds-brother of Aberdeen on 22 January 1663. [ABR]

MCKENZIE, THOMAS, brother of the Earl of Seaforth, a Captain of Mackay's Regiment in Danish Service in 1626, and in Swedish Service in 1629, was wounded in 1628 at Eckernfiord and Stralsund in Germany. [TGSI.VIII.87] [SAA.II.123]

MCKENZIE, Mr THOMAS, of Innerlawell, [Inbhir Lathail], Ross-shire, was granted lands in Ross-shire which formerly pertained to the late David Ross of Balnagowan, [Baile nan Gobhainn], on 9 June 1654. [RGSS.X.286]

MCKENZIE, THOMAS, son of Colin McKenzie of Kilroy, was apprenticed to Joseph Marjorybanks, a merchant in Edinburgh on 5 April 1671. [REA]

MCKENZIE, THOMAS, a labourer in Inverness, testament, 20 August 1677, Comm. Inverness. [NRS]

MCKENZIE, WILLIAM, from Ross-shire, a student at King's College, Aberdeen, in 1667-1677. [KCA]

MCKENZIE, WILLIAM, parson of Roskeen, [Ros Cuithne], a deed in 1685. [NRS.RD2.65.401]

MCKENZIE, ..., a sergeant in Donald Mackay's Company in Denmark, was killed at Stralsund, Mecklenburg, Germany, in 1628. [SAA.II.123]

MCKENZIE, Dr, was appointed as town physician of Inverness on 22 November 1680. [IMB.288]

MACKEY, ELIZABETH, possibly from Sutherland, a spinster in St Philip's parish, Barbados, probate 24 January 1700, Barbados. [RB.6.3.217]

MACKEY, ROBERT, a mariner aboard <u>HMS Hampton Court,</u> probate 1692 Prerogative Court of Canterbury. [TNA]

MACKIY, JAMES, died aboard <u>HMS Norfolk</u>, probate 1695 Prerogative Court of Canterbury. [TNA]

MCKILLICAN, ANDREW, a cordiner burgess of Inverness on 25 October 1667. [IMB.233], his spouse Janet Sutherland, testament, 26 August 1669 Comm. Inverness. [NRS]

MCKIMMIE, JANET, spouse of Donald McWilliam in Drunchardony, Wardlaw, testament, 15 December 1632 Comm. Inverness. [NRS]

MCKINNON, Dr DANIEL, born 1658, settled on Antigua, married Elizabeth Thomas, parents of Samuel. [St John's Town Library, Antigua, ms]; in Antigua in 1696, [TNA. Association Oath Roll]; petitioned for bail in Antigua on 11 June 1713, [RPCCol.vi.103/132]; was admitted as a burgess of Glasgow in 1717, [GBR]; died in 1720, probate 20 March 1720, Antigua.

MCKINNON, alias MCKEAN, JOHN, a tailor in Kedaini, Lithuania, between 1642 and 1650. [SCL.325]

MCKINNON, [MACFHINGHUIN], JOHN, possibly from Skye, Inverness-shire, was captured at the Battle of Dunbar in 1650, then transported to New England via London aboard the Unity in November 1650. [SG.35.3.136]

MCKINNON, JOHN, from the Isles, a student at King's College, Aberdeen, in 1655. [KCA]

MCKINNON, WILLIAM, from the Isles, a student at King's College, Aberdeen, in 1656. [KCA]

MCKNUCHTER, THOMAS, in Moortown, testament, 28 April 1676 Comm. Inverness. [NRS]

MCKYNICH, ALISTER, in Drumchardony, testament, 28 November 1668 Comm. Inverness. [NRS]

MCLACHLAN, DUGALL, and his family, in the Kirkton of Comar, Kiltarlity, [Cill Targhlain], Inverness-shire, in 1710. [NRS.CH1.2.29.3]

MCLAUCHLAN, MURIEL, spouse of Alexander McHucheon in Correbroch, Moy, testament, 13 November 1630 Comm. Inverness. [NRS]

MCLEAN, [MACGILLE EOIN], ALEXANDER, a merchant in Inverness in 1705, debtor of Patrick Fletcher, a merchant in Rotterdam, Holland. [NRS.AC8.57]

MCLEAN, ALLAN, from Mull, Inverness-shire, married Christine Morgan from Dunfermline, Fife, in the Scots Kirk, Rotterdam, on 16 January 1709. [GAR]

MCLEAN, ANGUS, a prisoner in Edinburgh Tolbooth, was transported via Leith to Barbados on 7 December 1665. [ETR.104]; possibly the 'Anguish Mackland' in St Andrew's, Overhill, probate 23 January 1684, Barbados. [RB.6.13]

MCLEAN, ANGUS, Captain in the Service of the States General of the United Netherlands, a commission from 1702 until 1710. [NRS.GD1.1062]

MCLEAN, CHARLES, a recusant and a burgess of Inverness, versus George Cuthbert, a merchant burgess of Inverness and others, then, Charles McArthur was to arrest him but was threatened by McLean, on 29 April 1653. [IMB.207]

MCLEAN, CHARLES, son of James McLean, a merchant in Inverness, a deed dated 1695. [NRS.RD3.83.763]

MCLEAN, DAVID, a juryman in an inquest in Inverness on 23 March 1686. [IMB.343]; was appointed as Lieutenant of a Militia Company, to protect Inverness from McDonald of Keppoch and his rebels, 3 September 1688. [IMB.7]

MCLEAN, DONALD, a burgess of Inverness, was sent to Sir Donald McDonald of Sleat, to obtain a donation towards the construction of a bridge at Inverness on 14 August 1682. [IMB.307]

MCLEAN, DONALD, a juryman in an inquest in Inverness on 23 March 1686. [IMB.343]

MCLEAN, FARQUHAR, youngest son of John McLean of Davoch gardoch, was admitted as a burgess and guild-brother of Inverness on 20 September 1686. [IMB.344]; was appointed as Lieutenant of a Militia Company, to protect Inverness from McDonald of Keppoch and his rebels, 3 September 1688. [IMB.7]

MCLEAN, HECTOR, a thief imprisoned in Inverness Tolbooth, was released in 1662. [TGSI.IX.119]

MCLEAN, HECTOR, a servant to the Viscount of Tarbet, was admitted as a burgess and guilds-brother of Edinburgh on 9 November 1687. [REB]

MCLEAN, J., a tacksman took the 'Oath of the Friends' thereby undertaking to financially support the McDonalds of Skye, subscribed at Duntuilme, [Dun Thuilm], Skye, on 1 February 1678. [TGSI.14.66]

MCLEAN, JAMES, a stent [tax] collector in Inverness on 19 April 1672. [IMB.252]; a juryman in an inquest in Inverness on 23 March 1686. [IMB.343]; a merchant, was appointed as Captain of a Militia Company, to protect a Inverness from McDonald of Keppoch and his rebels, 3 September 1688. [IMB.7]; a bailie of Inverness, a deed dated 1695. [NRS.RD4.76.421]

MCLEAN, JOHN, a mariner died aboard HMS Resolution, probate 1695 Prerogative Court of Canterbury. [TNA]

MCLEAN, LAUCHLAN, son of Alexander McLean of Wester Lynebulg, testament, 17 February 1669 Comm. Inverness. [NRS]

MCLENNAN, CALUM, from Stornaway, [Steornabhagh], Lewis, Outer Hebrides, a student at the Monastery at Ratisbon, Germany, in 1689, later at Wurzburg Germany from 1694. [SF.272][SIG.293]

MCLENNAN, DONALD, son of Allan McLennan in Glenelg, [Gleann Eilg], minister at Fearn from 1677 until his death in March 1689. [F.VII.56]

MACLENNAN, DONALD, born ca.1670 in Stornaway, was educated at Ratisbon around 1689, later at Wurzburg, became a priest in the West Highlands based in Knoydart, [Cnoideart], Inverness-shire], from 1703, died in Erfurt, Germany, in 1717. [TGSI.XLIV.100]

MCLENNAN, MURDOCH, and three children, in the Kirkton of Comar, Kiltarlity, Inverness-shire, in 1710. [NRS.CH1.2.29.3]

MCLEOD, AENEAS, of Cadboll, [Cadabal], Ross-shire, 1707/1708. [NRS.AC9.248/306]

MCLEOD, [MACLEOID], DANIEL, possibly from Sutherland, a militiaman of Captain Masson's Company in Barbados in 1679. [H2.43/193]

MCLEOD, DONALD, of Assynt, [Asainn], Sutherland, the younger, in 1643. [NRS.GD305.1.87.107]

MCLEOD, DONALD, a Captain of Colonel Aeneas Mackay's Regiment in Flanders, sasines in 1696. [NRS.RS36.VI.167/463]

MCLEOD, IAIN, born around 1645, son of Sir Norman McLeod of Bernaray and his wife Margaret McKenzie, tacksman of Contudsllich, [Conntulaich], Easter Ross, an advocate and a factor of the McLeod estates from 1700 to 1705, husband of Isobel McKenzie. [TGSI.XLIII.198]

MCLEOD, JOHN, of Harris, was admitted as a burgess and guildsbrother of Edinburgh on 13 September 1623. [REB]

MCLEOD, JOHN, possibly from the Outer Hebrides, was captured at the Siege of Worcester on 2 September 1651, was transported via London aboard the John and Sarah to New England in November 1651. [Suffolk Deeds, 1-56]; possibly settled in Lancaster, New England, by 1676. [LLNV.255]

MCLEOD, JOHN, son of Norman McLeod, was imprisoned in Inverness Tolbooth, a debtor of William McBean a burgess of Inverness, in April 1684. [IMB.321]

MCLEOD, JOHN, of Dunvegan, [Dun Mheagain], Skye, a deed in 1685. [NRS.RD2.55.508]

MCLEOD, JOHN, servant to George, Viscount of Tarbet, was admitted as a burgess and guilds-brother of Edinburgh on 29 June 1687. [REB]

MCLEOD, MALCOLM, probate, 4 February 1681 in Jamaica.

MCLEOD, MURDO, with two children, in South Uist, [Uibhist a Deas], Outer Hebrides, in 1703. [NRS.CH1.2.5.2]

MCLEOD, MURTLE, possibly from the Outer Hebrides, [Innse Gall], was captured at the Siege of Worcester on 2 September 1651, was transported via London aboard the John and Sarah bound for New England in December 1651. [Suffolk Deeds, 1-56]

MCLEOD, NEILL, of Assynt, a deed in 1694. [NRS.RD4.74.723]

MCLEOD, NICOLAS, a mariner aboard the <u>Beaufort</u> who died overseas, probate 1688 Prerogative Court of Canterbury. [TNA]

MCLEOD, PHILIP, in Christ Church parish, Barbados, probate 4 August 1687, Barbados.

MCLEOD, RODERICK, from Sutherland, a student at King's College, Aberdeen, in 1659. [KCA]

MCLEOD, RODERIC OG, son of Iain Breac McLeod the 18th Chief, died at Fortrose, Easter Ross, in 1699. [TGSI.XLIII.198]

MCLEOD, RONALD MOR, of Cillnacrack, Skye, a deed in 1685. [NRS.RD4.67.82]

MCLEOD, RORY, of Dunvegan, [Dun Bheagain], Skye, accepted Oliver Cromwell as his overlord, a bond dated 12 March 1655 subscribed at Sconce near Inverness. [TGSI.XLIV.74]

MCLEOD, WILLIAM, in Ferinlea, deceased in 1705. [TGSI.XLIV.314]

MCLEOD, ..., son of Neil McLeod, a sergeant of McKenzie's Company in Danish Service, was killed at Keil in 1628. [SAA.II.124]

MACLORGANE, ALLAN, minister at Tongue, [Tunga], Sutherland, around 1613. [F.VII.101]

MCMARTIN, MARTIN, of Letterfinlay, [Leitir Fhionlaigh], Inverness-shire, a prisoner in Inverness tolbooth was liberated by order of the Scottish Privy Council on 16 May 1684. [IMB.322]

MCMEIR, ALEXANDER, in Daviot, testament, 15 November 1630 Comm. Inverness. [NRS]

MCMURCHIE, DONALD, in Lochletter, testament, 8 July 1630 Comm. Inverness. [NRS]

MCNABB, JAMES, and his family, in Erchles, [Earghlais], Kiltarlity, Inverness-shire, in 1703. [NRS.CH1.2.5.2]

MCNEIL, ARCHIBALD, with two children, in Valslin, Barra, Outer Hebrides, in 1703. [NRS.CH1.2.5.2]

MCNEIL, DONALD, with two children, in Tangasdale, Barra, Outer Hebrides, in 1703. [NRS.CH1.2.5.2]

MCNEIL, DONALD, with two children, in Grim, Barra, Outer Hebrides, in 1703. [NRS.CH1.2.5.2]

MCNEILL, [MACNEILL], GALLIAN, of Barra, Uist, paid Ronald McDougall part of the money due by the Captain of Clan Ranald, for four horses, at Eriskay, [Eirisgeigh], on 29 January 1661. [NRS.GD201.1.71]

MCNEIL, JOHN, brother of the laird of Barra in the Outer Hebrides, with three children, in 1703. [NRS.CH1.2.5.2]

MCNEIL, JOHN, innkeeper at Dunvegan, Skye, in 1706. [TGSI.XLIV.315]

MCNEIL, MURDO, with two children, in Grim, Barra, Outer Hebrides, in 1703. [NRS.CH1.2.5.2]

MCNEIL, MURDO, with four children, in Vattersay, Barra, Outer Hebrides, in 1703. [NRS.CH1.2.5.2]

MCNEIL, MURDO, brother of the laird of Barra in the Outer Hebrides, with children, in 1703. [NRS.CH1.2.5.2]

MCNEIL, JOHN, with children, in the Kirkton of Comar, Kiltarlity, Inverness-shire, in 1703. [NRS.CH1.2.5.2]

MCNEILL, PAUL, in Drummuird, Laggan, testament, 11 June 1633 Comm. Inverness. [NRS]

MCNEILL, ROBERT, of Barra, at Kilphedir, [Cille Pheadair], Uist, paid Ronald McDougall part of the money due by the Captain of Clan Ranald, for four horses, on 15 November 1659. [NRS.GD201.1.66]

MCNEILL, RORIE, of Barra, at Eriskay, paid his uncle Donald McDonald of Moidart, 100 merks due for rent, on 9 May 1690. [NRS.GD201.1.22]; he was granted a Crown Charter dated 29 January

1688. [NRS.SIG1.137.48]; a deed dated 1695, [NRS.RD2.79.53]; with five children in 1703. [NRS.CH1.2.5.2]

MACNEILL, ..., of Barra, [Barraigh], a letter to the Earl of Glencairn dated 3 July 1653. [NRS.GD38.2.53]

MCNISHIE, JOHN, in Knocknebuy, testament, 7 June 1681 Comm. Inverness. [NRS]

MCNOYER, DONALD, [MAC-IAIN-UIDHIR], failed to appear before the High Burgh Court of Inverness on 10 January 1603. [ICB.3]

MCNOYER, THOMAS, was authorised to grant licenses to Highlanders and to residents of Inverness permitting them to sell whisky within Inverness-shire, on 25 May 1663. [IMB.215]

MCPHAILL, [MACPHAIL], DONALD, an alleged witch in Inverness in 1662. [TGSI.IX.119]

MCPHAILL, DONALD, in Innereine, testament, 19 February 1668 Comm. Inverness. [NRS]

MCPHAIL, FINDLAY, failed to appear before the High Burgh Court of Inverness on 10 January 1603. [ICB.3]

MCPHERSON, AGNES, spouse of Hector McLean in Tomatin, testament, 14 June 1676 Comm. Inverness. [NRS]

MCPHERSON, ALEXANDER, a messenger in Inverness in 1647. [IMB.195]

MCPHERSON, ALEXANDER, owned 2 acres in St Philip's parish, Barbados, in 1680. [H2/3]

MCPHERSON, ANGUS, settled in New England by 1656. [LLNV.255]

MCPHERSON, DONALD, of Delroddie, testament, 17 March 1669 Comm. Inverness. [NRS]

MCPHERSON, or GRANT, in Pitagown, testament, 17 October 1680 Comm. Inverness. [NRS]

MCPHERSON, ELIAS, second son of John McPherson of Inveressie, was apprenticed to Donald McPherson, a wright in Edinburgh, on 3 December 1684. [REA]

MCPHERSON, EWAN, in Essintulloch, Kingussie, testament, 45 December 1633 Comm. Inverness. [NRS]

MCQUEEN, JANET, in Rotterdam, Holland, by 1697. [NRS.RH4.17.1]

MCPHERSON, JOHN, born 1656, an Episcopalian deacon and schoolmaster of Thurso was ordained as a minister of the Church of Scotland in 1697, minister at Farr from 1697 until his death on 28 January 1726. Father of Isobel. [F.VII.106]

MCPHERSON, JOHN, from Inverness, a student at King's College, Aberdeen, in 1677. [KCA]

MCPHERSON, JOHN, of Dalvedie, was admitted as a burgess of Inverness on 3 December 1687. [NRS.NRAS.bundle 581]

MCPHERSON, KATHERINE, daughter of Donald McPherson in Shirromer, testament, 18 April 1676 Comm. Inverness. [NRS]

MCPHERSON, LACHLAN, of Torcastle, the laird of McIntosh, disposed of the lands of Obstell to William Duff the Provost of Inverness, a sasine dated in May 1693. [NRS.NRAS.103/4]

MCPHERSON, LAUCHLAN, of Pitmean, testament, 30 October 1669 Comm. Inverness. [NRS]

MCPHERSON, MALCOLM, in Phoynes, testament, 12 March 1678 Comm. Inverness. [NRS]

MACPHERSON, [MAC A PHERSOIN], Mr MARTIN, minister of Kilmuir, [Cill Mhoir], Ross-shire, was attacked by Captain John McDonald of Clan Ranald and his men who destroyed property and crops, and stealing 54 cattle, 68 sheep and lambs, 13 horses, and utensils, in 1658, the courts seem to have failed to punish McDonald or to retrieve the stolen assets. [TGSI.14.70]

MCPHERSON, NEILL, in Kinloch, testament, 11 September 1666 Comm. Inverness. [NRS]

MCPHERSON, NEIL, from Inverness, and Janet Fordue from London, were married in Rotterdam, Holland, on 20 June 1706. [GAR]

MCPHERSON, WILLIAM, of Wester Craig, granted his brother Donald McPherson half the lands of Wester Craig, Strathnairn, Daviot, Inverness-shire, on 11 July 1665. [NRS.NRAS.171.bundle 542]

MCPHERSON, WILLIAM, in Bellachroan, testament, 11 March 1678 Comm. Inverness. [NRS]

MCQUEEN, [MAC SHUIBHE], 'AMOS', was captured at the Siege of Worcester on 2 September 1651, then transported via London aboard the John and Sarah bound for New England in December 1651, landed there in February 1652. [Suffolk Deeds.1/5-6]

MCQUEEN, Mr ARCHIBALD, authorised Donald McDonald of Moydart, [Muideart], Inverness-shire, to pay £100 Scots for the

maintenance of Donald McQueen at college, dated at Cillwirrie, Durness, Sutherland, on 29 April 1659. [NRS.GD201.3.9]

MACQUEEN, ARCHIBALD, a soldier of Captain Scott's Company of Militia in Barbados in 1679. [H2.191]

MCQUEEN, CHARLES, from Inverness, settled in Veere, Zeeland, in 1659. [ZA; A.S.V.inventory 920]

MCQUEEN, CHRISTIAN, spouse of Finlay McClay in Pitmean, testament, 30 October 1669 Comm. Inverness. [NRS]

MCQUEEN, DONALD, in Corribroch, was denounced as a rebel in 1619. [RPCS.XI.565]

MCQUEIN, DONALD, of Cluni, [Cluainidh], gave a bond of twenty pounds Scots towards the construction of the bridge at Inverness, on 10 July 1682. [IMB.305]

MCQUEEN, ELSPET, spouse of James Mackay in Tornagaven, testament, 31 July 1678 Comm. Inverness. [NRS]

MCQUEEN, GEORGE, was captured at the Siege of Worcester on 2 September 1651, then transported via London aboard the John and Sarah bound for New England in December 1651, landed there in February 1652. [Suffolk Deeds.1/5-6]

MCQUEEN, SWEIN, of Raik, [Roag], was denounced as a rebel in 1619. [RPCS.XI.565]

MCQUEEN, SWEYNE, in Roybeg, Moy, testament, 22 January 1633 Comm. Inverness. [NRS]

MCQUEEN, SWYNE, in Inverness, formerly tacksman of the King's Mill there, a deed in 1694. [NRS.RD3.82.16/19]

MCRAE, ALEXANDER, a mariner aboard HMS Dartmouth probate 1695 Prerogative Court of Canterbury. [TNA]

MCRAE, ALEXANDER, born in Kilmorack, [Cill Mhoraig]; Inverness-shire, on 24 February 1672, son of Reverend John McRae, an Episcopalian minister, was educated at Douai, Flanders, Tournai, Flanders, and Prague, Bohemia, returned to Scotland in 1703, a Jesuit priest in Dingwall, Easter Ross, in 1707, died at Douai, Flanders. [NRS.CH1.2.30.1.4] [NLS.ms68.31] [IR.XXIV.87]

MACRAE, DONALD, minister at Urray and Tarradale, from 1645 until 1656 then in Kintail. He was chaplain to the Earl of Seaforth's regiment raised in support of King Charles I. [F.7.49]

MCRAE. DONALD, from Ross-shire, a student at King's College, Aberdeen, in 1667. [KCA]

MCRAE, DUNCAN, in Inverinate, Kintail, Wester Ross, a deed dated 1695. [NRS.RD2.79.26]

MCRAE, [MACKRAY], Mr WILLIAM, was admitted as a burgess and guilds-brother of Aberdeen on 28 June 1650. [ABR]

MCRAE, [MACRATH], Mr JOHN, minister at Dingwall, Easter Ross, was granted various properties in Dingwall on 12 August 1652. [RGSS.X.16]

MACRAW, JOHN, schoolmaster in Dingwall, Ross and Cromarty in 1664. [Inverness and Dingwall Presbytery Records, 306]; later as minister at Dingwall, was granted land and property in Dingwall on 12 August 1652. [RGSS.X.16]

MCROBBY, ANDREW, the kirk officer of Wardlaw, testament, 18 February 1678 Comm. Inverness. [NRS]

MCROBBY, WILLIAM, in Lairg, testament, 19 July 1677 Comm. Inverness. [NRS]

MCRORIE, JAMES, in Dedham, New England, in 1662. [LLNV.254]

MACRORIE, [MAC RUARIDH], alias MACLEAN, JOHN, linked with the trial of witches in Inverness in 1662. [TGSI.IX.118]

MCRORIE, JOHN, in Corrivernoch, testament, 16 June 1668 Comm. Inverness. [NRS]

MCRORIE, JOHN, and his wife Margaret Munro, in Comar, Kiltarlity, Inverness-shire, in 1679. [IR.XXIV.82]

MCSLIGACH, WILLIAM, in Achnacloich, testament, 10 June 1680 Comm. Inverness. [NRS]

MCSORLE, FINLAY, in Gortannaries of Kinrara, testament, 21 October 1680 Comm. Inverness. [NRS]

MCTAVISH, WILLIAM, in Auchnagairine, testament, 10 November 1669 Comm. Inverness. [NRS]

MCVIC ROB, JAMES, in Urray or Kilchrist, participated in the rebellion under James Graham, Marquis of Montrose, in 1649. [SHS.24.159]

MCVIRRICH, [MAC MHARAIS] FINDLAY, failed to appear before the High Burgh Court of Inverness on 10 January 1603. [ICB.3]

MCWARRONICH, JANET, daughter of John McWarronich in Inverness, testament, 16 April 1633 Comm. Inverness. [NRS]

MCWILLIAM, DUNCAN, in Cribinclay, testament, 18 May 1666 Comm. Inverness. [NRS]

MCWILLIAM, FARQUHAR, and his wife Beatrix, in Comar, Kiltarlity, Inverness-shire, in 1679. [IR.XXIV.82]

MCWILLIAM [MAC UILLEIM] VICCONNELL ROY, JOHN RIACH, in Urray or Kilchrist, participated in the rebellion under James Graham, Marquis of Montrose, in 164+9. [SHS.24.159]

MCWIRRICH, DONALD, in Raitt, testament, 22 March 1631 Comm. Inverness.[NRS]

MCWIRRICH, WILLIAM, a merchant in Inverness, raised letters of horning against Donald Beaton, a merchant in Dingwall, Easter Ross, re unpaid debts on 11 June 1700. [NRS.GD23.5.148]

MCWEYNISH, DONALD, a witness in an inquest in Inverness on 23 March 1686.
[IMB.343]

MCYELMICH, THOMAS, servant of bailiff Fraser, a witness in an inquest in Inverness on 23 March 1686. [IMB.343]

MALCOLM, or MACGILLIECALLUM, JOHN, minister at Urray and Tarradale, from 1605 until 1635. [F.7.49]

MALCOLMSON, JOHN, minister at Wray, and Isabella McKenzie his wife, disposed of land in Dingwall, Ross-shire, to Mr Murdoch McKenzie in April 1638. [NRS.GD93.199]

MAN, WILLIAM, from Ross-shire, a student at King's College, Aberdeen, in 1661-1663 [KCA]

MANSON, GEORGE, a Lance Corporal of Monro's Company in Danish Service around 1628. [SAA.II.125]

MANSON, JOHN, in Dornoch, Sutherland, paid his Hearth Tax in 1694. [NRS.E69.23.1.3]

MANSON, WILLIAM, in Dornoch, Sutherland, paid his Hearth Tax in 1694. [NRS.E69.23.1.3]

MARCUS, ALEXANDER, a packer in Inverness in 1645. [MCM.I.47]

MARNOCH, GILBERT, a debtor for the stent in Kirk Street, Inverness, in 1647. [IMB.194]

MARQUIS, ELSPETH, a brewer in Inverness, was fined for breaking the statutes on beer, on 25 January 1613. [ICB.103]

MARQUIS, FINLAY, a refractory tanner in Inverness in 1631. [RPCS.IV.295]

MARQUIS, JOHN, a skipper had failed to pay his anchorage dues for 1646-1647 in Inverness, was fined twenty pounds, on 12 October 1646. [IMB.192]

MATHESON, JOHN, a sutler in Mackay's Regiment in Denmark from 1626. [SAA.II.131]

MATTHEW, MARGARET, spouse of Andrew Schaw a merchant burgess of Inverness, testament, 29 June 1668 Comm. Inverness. [NRS]

MAXWELL, GABRIEL, minister at Kildonan in 1641. [F.7.90]

MAXWELL, JAMES, skipper of the James of Dunrossness in 1674. [NRS.RD4.warrant.1110]

MAY, JOHN, failed to appear before the High Burgh Court of Inverness on 10 January 1603. [ICB.3]

MELDRUM, DUNCAN, in Inverness, testament, 9 May 1666 Comm. Inverness. [NRS]

MERCHANT, THOMAS, failed to appear before the High Burgh Court of Inverness on 10 January 1603. [ICB.3]

MERCHISTON, RICHARD, graduated MA from Edinburgh University i 1595, minister at Edzell, Angus, from 1597 until 1611, then at Bowe [Bagair], Caithness, from 1612 until 1633 when he was drowned in the Water of Wick by local Roman Catholics in revenge for mutilatin the statue of St Fergus, the patron saint of Wick. Father of David an Thomas. [F.VII.114]

MIDDLETON, JAMES, master of the Joan of Inverness, arrived in Inverness on 3 July 1689 from Holland. [NRS.E72.11.14]

MILL, ANDREW, a soldier from Caithness, [Gallaibh], married Catherine Adam from Leith, in Schiedam, the Netherlands on 26 April 1635. [Schiedam Marriage Register]

MILL, ANDREW, in Dornoch, Sutherland, paid his Hearth Tax in 1694. [NRS.E69.23.1.3]

MILLER, PATRICK, in Buntait, testament, 22 November 1669 Comm. Inverness. [NRS]

MILNE, JAMES, schoolmaster at Fort William, Inverness-shire, in 1699. [NRS.RD2.82.623]

MIRRIE, MARTIN, a burgess of Inverness, testament, 10 October 1667 Comm. Inverness. [NRS]

MOIR, JAMES, imprisoned in Inverness Tolbooth, was liberated by Alexander Blackwood another prisoner there, on 4 February 1667. [IMB.231]

MOIR, MARGARET, daughter of Donald Moir, and spouse to John McKurkullin in Tiubeg, [An Taobh Beag], Sutherland, testament, July 1663, Comm. Caithness. [NRS]

MONCREIFF, CHRISTIAN, spouse of George Cuming a burgess of Inverness, testament, 13 October 1634 Comm. Inverness. [NRS]

MOWAT, ALEXANDER, from Ross-shire, a student at King's College, Aberdeen, in 1661. [KCA]

MUNRO, ALEXANDER, born 1605, son of Hector Munro of Milnton of Katewell, [Ciadail], Ross-shire, a dyer in Inverness, a teacher in Strathnaver, [Srath Nabhair], later minister at Tongue, [Tunga], Sutherland, from 1634 until his death in 1653. Husband of Janet Cumming, parents of Hew his successor, John minister at Alness, Donald schoolmaster in Alness, Hector, Agnes, and Christian. [F.VII.101]

MONRO, ALEXANDER, from Ross-shire, a student at King's College, Aberdeen, in 1660. [KCA]

MONRO, ALEXANDER, from Inverness, a student at King's College, Aberdeen, in 1665. [KCA]

MUNRO, ALEXANDER, a Lieutenant Colonel of Lord Douglas's Regiment, a deed in 1670, [NRS.RD4.26.503]; Lieutenant Colonel of the Earl of Dunfermline's Regiment in France, a deed in 1676, [NRS.RD4.39.199]; a Captain of Lord George Douglas's Regiment in France, a deed in 1681. [NRS.RD2.54.535]

MONRO, ALEXANDER, a skipper in Inverness, in 1681. [RPCS.XI.530]

MONRO, ANDREW, an Ensign of Monro's Company in Danish Service in 1628. [SAA.II.125]

MUNRO, ANDREW, a Captain of Mackay's Regiment in Danish Service in 1626, was killed in a duel on Fermern Island, Denmark, in 1629. [TGSI.VIII.187] [SAA.II.127]

MONRO, ANDREW, the younger of Kincraig, [Ceann na Creige], Inverness-shire, was admitted as a burgess of Aberdeen on 8 December 1627. [ABR]

MUNRO, ANDREW, a Captain of Mackay's Regiment in Danish Service in 1626, in Swedish Service in 1629, was killed at Oldenburg, Germany, in September 1629. [TGSI.VIII.188] [SAA.II.131]

MONRO, ANDREW, from Ross-shire, a student at King's College, Aberdeen in 1647. [KCA]

MONRO, ANDREW, participated as a Captain in the Royalist uprising under James Graham, Marquis of Montrose, into England 1649. [SHS.24.159][NRS.CH2.91.1]

MUNRO, Mr ANDREW, minister in Thurso, Caithness, in 1658, reference. [RGSS.X.634]

MONRO, ANDREW, from Ross-shire, a student at King's College, Aberdeen, in 1659. [KCA]

MONRO, ANDREW, [1], from Ross-shire, a student at King's College, Aberdeen, in 1674. [KCA]

MONRO, ANDREW, [2], from Ross-shire, a student at King's College, Aberdeen, in 1674. [KCA]

MUNRO, ANDREW, a wright in Culernie in 1682. [SHS.24.114]

MUNRO, CHARLES, husband of Janet Sutherland, granted letters of redemption in favour of John Ferguson, a merchant burgess of Tain, Easter Ross, on 28 May 1623.[NRS.GD/1.34]

MUNRO, DAVID, a Major of Mackay's Regiment in Danish Service in 1626, in Swedish Service in 1629, 'was scorched by powder at Eckernfiord'. [TGSI.VIII.186]

MUNRO, DAVID, an officer of Mackay's Regiment in Danish Service in 1626, in Swedish Service in 1629, was wounded at Oldenburg, Germany, in September 1627. [TGSI.VIII.188] [SAA.II.126]

MONRO, DAVID, from Keatuall, [Ciadail], Ross-shire, admitted participating in the Royalist uprising led by James Graham, the Marquis of Montrose, into England and at the Siege of Inverness in 1649. [SHS.24.157] [NRS.CH2.92.1]

MONRO, DAVID, from Ross-shire, a student at King's College, Aberdeen, in 1661. [KCA]

MUNRO, DAVID, fourth son of John Munro of Pitlundie, minister at Kilmuir Easter, then at Latheron until deposed in 1649, finally at Lairg from 1663, husband of Barbara Gray. [F.7.92]

MONRO, DONALD, from Ross-shire, a student at King's College, Aberdeen, in 1646. [KCA]

MONRO, DONALD, from Alness, admitted participating in the Royalist uprising led by James Graham, the Marquis of Montrose, into England and in the north of Scotland in 1649. [SHS.24.157] [NRS.CH2.92.1]

MONRO, DONALD, in Culcabock, testament, 18 February 1669 Comm. Inverness. [NRS]

MONRO, DONALD, a skipper in Inverness, in 1681. [RPCS.XI.530]

MUNRO, FARQUHAR, a Sergeant of Mackay's Regiment in Danish Service in 1626, in Swedish Service in 1629, was killed at Oldenburg, Germany. [TGSI.VIII.188][SAA.II.124]

MUNRO, GEORGE, minister at Fearn and Tarbet, [Tairbeart], Ross-shire, until 1616. [F.VII.56]

MUNRO, GEORGE, minister at Urquhart from 1642 until 1656. [F.7.46]

MUNRO, GEORGE, from Caithness, a student at King's College, Aberdeen, in 1673-1675-1677. [KCA]

MUNRO, Sir GEORGE, of Culrain, [Cul Rathain], Sutherland, appointed Donald Sinclair, Master of Reay, as his factor of lands in the parishes of Durness, [Diurrnis], and Kirkboll, Sutherland, on 25 April 1678. [NRS.GD84.1.4.10]; granted George Mackay, Lord Reay, a tack [lease] of the lands and baronies of Farr, Kintail, and Durness in Sutherland, on 23 February 1693. [NRS.GD84.1.4.10]

MUNRO, HECTOR, of Daan, second son of William Munto minister at Cullicudden, graduated MA at St Andrews University in 1610, minister at Edderton from 1614 until 1665, husband of [1] Euphemia Ross, [2] Isabel Davidson. [F.VII.53]

MUNRO, HECTOR, of Foulis, [Foghlais], Ross-shire, an officer of Mackay's Regiment in Danish Service in 1626, in Swedish Service in 1629, a Colonel in Swedish Service in 1630s, later a Colonel in Dutch Service. [TGSI.VIII.187][RGS.9.112]

MONRO, HECTOR, of Coul, a sergeant of Thomas Mackenzie's Company who was wounded at Oldenburg, Germany, in September 1627. [SAA.II.124]

MONRO, HECTOR, of Clyne, Sutherland, was admitted as a burgess of Aberdeen on 27 October 1628. [ABR]

MONRO, HECTOR, of Foulis, a student at King's College, Aberdeen, in 1673. [KCA]

MONRO, HECTOR, of Little Altes, a marriage contract with Elizabeth McKenzie, daughter of John McKenzie of Davoch Cairn, dated 9 December 1681. [NRS.NRAS.143.Bundle 30]

MONRO, HECTOR, servant of baillie Fraser, a witness in an inquest in Inverness on 23 March 1686. [IMB.343]

MONRO, HECTOR, son of Daniel Monro in Sutherland, was apprenticed to David Christy a periwig maker in Edinburgh on 28 August 1689. [REA]

MONRO, HEW, drill master of Inverness, was discharged on 13 May 1644. [IMB.183]

MUNRO, HUGH, a student at King's College, Aberdeen, in 1650. [KCA]

MONRO, HUGH, probably from Ross-shire, was captured at the Battle of Dunbar on 2 September 1650, was transported via London aboard the John and Sarah bound for New England on 8 December 1650, landed in Boston by 28 February 1651. [NWI.I.151]

MUNRO, HEW, born ca.1637, graduated MA from King's College, Aberdeen, in 1657, minister at Durness, [Diurnis], Sutherland, from 1663 until his death between 1701 and 1703. [F.VII.102]

MONRO, HEW, son of Teniach, from Alness, admitted taking part in the Royalist uprising led by James Graham, Marquis of Montrose, into England and at the Siege of Inverness in 1649. [SHS.24.157][NRS.CH2.92.1]

MONRO, HUGH, from Ross-shire, a student at King's College, Aberdeen, in 1668-1676. [KCA]

MONRO, HUGH, of Eriboll, [Earabl], Sutherland, disposed of the lands of Eriboll, to his son John Monro as part of the marriage contract between the said John and Rachel McKay, eldest daughter of Angus McKay of Bighouse, dated 27 January 1688. [NRS.GD84.1.19.14]

MONRO, Captain IAN, a soldier in Denmark around 1627-1628. [NRS.GD84.159][SAA.II.132]

MONRO, JANET, relict of Sir Robert Monro of Foulis, a deed in 1685. [NRS.RD2.66.425]

MUNROE, JOHN, a soldier of 1st Company of Cockburn's Regiment in Swedish Service in 1609. [SIS.217]

MUNRO, JOHN, of Obisdell, [Obasdal], Ross-shire, a Captain of Mackay's Regiment in Danish Service in 1626, in Swedish Service in 1629, later Colonel of a Scottish Regiment. [TGSI.VIII.187][SAA.II.125]

MUNRO, JOHN, of Assynt, [Asaint], Sutherland, a Captain, later a Lieutenant Colonel, of Mackay 's Regiment in Danish Service in 1626, in Swedish Service in 1629. [TGSI.VIII.187][SAA.II.125]

MONRO, JOHN, in Cuinaskeah, Kiltearn, admitted participating as a Lieutenant in the Royalist uprising led by James Graham,

Marquis of Montrose into England and at the Siege of Inverness in 1649. [SHS.24.157][NRS.CH2.92.1]

MONRO, JOHN, Lieutenant Colonel of Fraser's Dragoons in 1646 during the Wars of the Three Kingdoms.

MONRO, JOHN, probably from Ross-shire, was captured at the Battle of Dunbar on 2 September 1650, was transported via London aboard the John and Sarah bound for New England on 8 December 1650, landed in Boston by 28 February 1651. [NWI.I.151][Suffolk Deeds, I.5-6]

MUNRO, JOHN, son of Major Hector Munro of Coul, [A'Chuil], Ross-shire, and his wife Isabella Ross, minister at Farr, Sutherland, from 1663. Husband of Isobel Anderson, parents of William, Thomas, and David. [F.VII.106]

MONRO, JOHN, from Sutherland, a student at King's College, Aberdeen, in 1665. [KCA]

MUNRO, JOHN, a maltman, in Inverness on 25 October 1667. [IMB.233]

MONRO, JOHN, from Inverness, a student at King's College, Aberdeen, in 1667. [KCA]

MUNRO, JOHN, a 'chakster' in Inverness on 25 October 1667. [IMB.233]

MONRO, JOHN, from Ross-shire, a student at King's College, Aberdeen, in 1668-1670. [KCA]

MUNRO, JOHN, from Caithness, a student at King's College, Aberdeen, in 1673. [KCA]

MONRO, JOHN, in Daviot, testament, 12 August 1678 Comm. Inverness. [NRS]

MONRO, JOHN, schoolmaster of Kiltarlity, Inverness-shire, in 1677. [SHS.24.77]; late tutor to Lord Lovat, was appointed schoolmaster of Inverness Grammar School on 28 March 1682, resigned in May 168! [IMB.303/325]

MUNRO, JOHN, a soldier in Captain Helm's Company of Militia in Barbados in 1679. [H2.153]

MUNRO, JOHN, of Clyne, [Chlin], Sutherland, a Captain of Strathnaver's Regiment in 1689.

MUNRO, JOHN, a merchant in Wick, Caithness, a deed dated 1695. [NRS.RD4.77.490]

MUNRO, JOHN, a tailor in Tain, a deed dated 1695. [NRS.RD4.77.611]

MONRO, KENNETH, of Seaforth, a student at King's College, Aberdeen, in 1650. [KCA]

MUNRO, MARIE, spouse of James Sutherland in Inverness, testament, 2 August 1630 Comm. Inverness. [NRS]

MUNRO, NEIL, of Findon, a marriage contract with Janet McKenzie, relict of William Cuthbert of Auld Castlehill, dated 5 February 1627. [NRS.NRAS.143.bundle30]

MONRO, NEIL, of Findon, [Fionndun], Ross-shire, admitted taking part in a Royalist uprising led by James Graham, Marquis of Montrose, into England in 1649. [SHS.24.157][NRS.CH2.92.1]

MUNRO, NEIL, fiar of Swardell, [Suardal], Ross-shire, about to go abroad, appointed John Munro of Foulis, Robert Munro of Clynes, Hector Munro of Swardell, father of the said Neil, factor of the lands of Swardell, witnesses were Alexander Macintosh in Assynt, Hugh Munro son of George Munro in Alness, and John Munro in Dergon, registered in the Sheriff Court Books of Ross on 31 July 1684. [SRS.Munro of Foulis Writs]

MONRO, REBECCA, daughter of Sir Robert Monro of Foulis, Ross-shire, and spouse of Colin Robertson of Kindeis, [Cinn Deis], Ross-shire, a deed in 1685. [NRS.RD2.66.425]

MUNRO, ROBERT, of Creichmor, third son of John Munro of Coul and his wife Katherine Vass, minister at Urquhart from 1574 until 1638, husband of Christian Munro. [F.7.46]

MUNRO, ROBERT, minister at Edderton, [Eadardun], Ross-shire, in 1607. [F.VII.53]

MUNRO, ROBERT, minister at Durness from 1603 until 1632, husband of Elspet Munro, parents of Hector Munro. [F.VII.101]

MONRO, ROBERT, of Foulis, Ross-shire, was admitted as a burgess of Aberdeen on 14 August 1619. [ABR]

MUNRO, ROBERT, of Coul, son of William Munro and his wife Isobel Thornton, minister at Kiltearn from 1589, then at Farr from 1619 until 1635. Husband of Elizabeth Munro, parents of Hector, Elizabeth, and Margaret. [F.VII.106]

MUNRO, ROBERT, of Contullich, [Conntulaich], Ross-shire, of the King of France's Regiment of Guards before 1626, a Colonel in Danish Service, in Swedish Service in Germany around 1634, served in the Parliament's army during 1642. [TGSI.VIII.187] [SAA.II.127]; possibly the Colonel General Robert Monro, 'in command of the Scottish expedition', was admitted as a burgess of Aberdeen on1 September 1640. [ABR]

MONRO, ROBERT, from Alness, admitted participating in the Royalist uprising led by James Graham, the Marquis of Montrose, into England and at the Siege of Inverness in 1649. [SHS.24.157] [NRS.CH2.92.1]

MUNRO, ROBERT, son of Hector Munro and his wife Anne Fraser, of Foulis, Ross-shire, an officer in Danish Service in 1627, later in Swedish Service as Colonel of a Dutch Regiment; was granted various lands in Inverness-shire, and Sutherland formerly held by his brother Sir George Munro, on 23 August 1652. [RGSS.X.17][SAA.II.126]

MUNRO, ROBERT, from Ross-shire, a student at King's College, Aberdeen, in 1650. [KCA]

MONRO, ROBERT, from Ross-shire, a student at the Scots College in Rome in 1668. [RSC.118]

MONRO, ROBERT, from Caithness, a student at King's College, Aberdeen, in 1676. [KCA]

MONRO, ROBERT, of Foulis, Ross-shire, Captain of Lord Strathnaver's Regiment in 1689.

MONRO, THOMAS, Quartermaster Sergeant of Monro of Obiswell's Company in Denmark around 1628. [SAA.II.126]

MUNRO, THOMAS, a soldier in Captain Burton's Company in Militia in Barbados in 1679. [H2.153]; a militiaman in Barbados in 1689. [H2.152]

MONRO, WILLIAM, a burgess of Tain, Ross-shire, was admitted as a burgess of Aberdeen on 2 September 1629. [ABR]

MONRO, WILLIAM, in Inverness on 25 October 1667. [IMB.233]

MONRO, WILLIAM, from Ross-shire, a student at King's College, Aberdeen, in 1669. [KCA]

MORE, ALLISTER, a debtor for the stent in Kirk Street, Inverness in 1647. [IMB.194]

MORE, FINLAY, in Newtoun, testament, 8 December 1666 Comm. Inverness. [NRS]

MORE, RONALD, a source of timber for the bridge at Inverness in January 1654. [IMB.208]

MORRISON, RODERICK, a merchant in Stornaway, Lewis, a debtor of John Morrison, a writer, [lawyer], in Edinburgh, in 1705. – [NRS.AC9.123]

MOWAT, MAGNUS, of Boquhollie, disposed of his lands in Harpsdale, Halkirk, Caithness, to George, Earl of Caithness, and his spouse Jean Gordon, on 8 June 1605. [NRS.GD96.321]

MOWAT, MAGNUS, in Uybuster testament, 14 January 1662, Comm. Caithness. [NRS]

MOWAT, WILLIAM, in Freswick, Caithness, testament dated 9 July 1661, Comm. Caithness. [NRS]

MULLOCH, JOHN, testament, 14 September 1631 Comm. Inverness. [NRS]

MURRAY, ALEXANDER, in Blindserie, testament, dated 17 February 1663, Comm. Caithness. [NRS]

MURRAY, BARBARA, in Dornoch, Sutherland, paid her Hearth Tax in 1694. [NRS.E69.23.1.3]

MURRAY, DONALD, a merchant burgess of Perth and of Inverness, testament, 25 January 1633 Comm. Inverness. [NRS]

MURRAY, DONALD, son of Donald Murray in Inverness, was apprenticed to James McIvain a cook in Edinburgh on 9 Augus 1665. [REA]

MURRAY, FRANCIS, son of Robert Murray a merchant in Thurso, was apprenticed to Alexander McKenzie a tailor in Edinburgh on 22 July 1646, when he died Francis was transferred to James Paterson on 11 August 1647. [REA]

MURRAY, HELEN, in Dornoch, Sutherland, paid her Hearth Tax in 1694. [NRS.E69.23.1.3]

MURRAY, JAMES, eldest son of John Murray of Pennyland, and his spouse Elizabeth Wemyss, were granted various lands in Caithness, formerly held by Sir James Sinclair and his spouse Katherine Murray, also by Sir James Sinclair of Murkill, on 1 January 1658. [RGSS.X.634]

MURRAY, JOHN, servant of the Bishop of Ross, was admitted as a burgess and guilds-brother of Aberdeen on 3 December 1635. [ABR]

MURRAY, MURDOCH, in Dornoch, Sutherland, paid his Hearth Tax in 1694. [NRS.E69.23.1.3]

MURRAY, PATRICK, from Caithness, a student at King's College, Aberdeen, in 1675. [KCA]

MURRAY, Mr PATRICK, the Admiral Depute of Caithness, participated in the saving and salvage of the Pelsor of Amsterdam in the Pentland Firth in 1706. [NRS.AC9.239]

MURRAY, WILLIAM, in Dornoch, Sutherland, paid his Hearth Tax in 1694. [NRS.E69.23.1.3]

MURRAY, WILLIAM, the younger, in Dornoch, Sutherland, paid his Hearth Tax in 1694. [NRS.E69.23.1.3]

NAIRNE, JOHN, in Tullochcruben, testament, 30 August 1666 Comm. Inverness. [NRS]

NAIRNE, PATRICK, in Tullochcruben, testament, 5 September 1666 Comm. Inverness. [NRS]

NEILSON, ALEXANDER, a cramer [pedlar] in Inverness on 1 August 1670. [IMB.242]; a cramer [pedlar], complained to the burgh council that some hucksters were selling goods at the Cross on the basis they were militia-men and were entitled to trade there, on 18 December 1671. [IMB.250]

NEILSON, JOHN, a Notary Public in Inverness in 1662. [TGSI.IX.119-120]

NEILSON, WILLIAM, a councillor of Inverness in 1642. [IMB.181]; NEILSON, WILLIAM, in Dornoch, paid his Hearth Tax in 1694. [NRS.E69.23.1.3]

NICOLASSON, MALLIE, wife of John Sinclair in the Boigis, testament, January 1663, Comm. Caithness. [NRS]

NICOLSON, ALEXANDER, was contracted to repair the pier, and to be paid twenty pounds in advance and a further twenty pounds on completion of the work, also, he was to be admitted as a freeman of his trade and a burgess of Inverness, 9 September 1678. [IMB.278]

NICOLSON, JOHN, a shoemaker in Thurso, testament, July 1664, Comm. Caithness. [NRS]

NICOLSON, ROBERT, a mason in Inverness, repaired the Town House in June 1675, also, in April 1677. [IMB.262/272]

NIVEN, WILLIAM, Master of the Music School in Inverness, was admitted as a burgess and guilds-brother of Inverness on 27 September 1686. [IMB.345]

NOBLE, DONALD, in Morill, and his wife Margaret McGillivray, testament, 9 October 1678 Comm. Inverness. [NRS]

OGILVIE, ALEXANDER, from Ross-shire, a student at King's College, Aberdeen, in 1663-1664. [KCA]

OGILVIE, MARGARET, spouse of Neil Grant in Duthell, testament, 25 March 1678 Comm. Inverness. [NRS]

OGSTON, ANDREW, born 1568 in Buchan, minister at Canisby, Caithness, from 1601 until his death on 31 March 1650. [F.VII.116]

OIGSTONE, BARBARA, wife of David Sinclair in Olrick, Caithness, testament, 31 May 1664, Comm. Caithness. [NRS]

OLIPHANT, WILLIAM, in Balchroan, testament, 16 March 1678 Comm. Inverness. [NRS]

ORMSLIE, GEORGE, a mariner in Thurso, Caithness, husband of [1] Bathen ....., [2] Margaret Purdie, father of Janet Ormslie, a sasine in 1661. [NRS.RS20.2.62]

OSWALD, JAMES, from Caithness, a student at King's College, Aberdeen, in 1670. [KCA]

PAPE, CHARLES, from Ross-shire, a student at King's College, Aberdeen, in 1668.-1670. [KCA]

PAPE, HUGH, schoolmaster of Alness, [Alanais], Ross-shire, deeds from 1673 to 1675. [NRS.RD4.33.679; RD2.38.702; RD2.40.417]

PATERSON, ALEXANDER, a former baillie of Inverness, who had fallen into poverty, was granted a pension of forty merks yearly by the burgh council on 11 June 1638; .was collect stent money to finance a Gaelic church in Inverness on 14 June 1649. [IMB.175/201]

PATERSON, THOMAS, from Inverness, a student at King's College, Aberdeen, in 1669. [KCA]

PATERSON, WILLIAM, the elder, failed to appear before the High Burgh Court of Inverness on 10 January 1603. [ICB.3]

PATERSON, WILLIAM, the younger, a burgess of Inverness, testament 25 June 1631, Comm. Inverness. [NRS]

PATERSON, WILLIAM, a bailie of Inverness in 1642. [IMB.181]; was appointed stent [tax] collector for the Briggait of Inverness on 14 December 1644. [IMB.186]

PATERSON, W., of Inches, a councillor of Inverness in 1642. [IMB.181]

PATERSON, WILLIAM, a councillor in Inverness, took the Test Oath on 26 September 1682. [IMB.310]; was appointed as Captain of a Militia Company, to protect Inverness from McDonald of Keppoch and his rebels, 3 September 1688. [IMB.7]

PAUL, ROBERT, a shoemaker burgess of Inverness, was accused of threatening baillie Robertson to release John McFarquhar a prisoner, in April 1671 with assistance of Robert Winchester, Robert Paul had his burgess rights withdrawn. [IMB.247]

PHAILL, CHRISTIAN, an alleged witch in Inverness in 1662. [TGSI.IX.119]

POLSON, ANGUS, was appointed assistant toll-keeper of the Inverness bridge on 13 August 1683. [IMB.318]

POLSON, DAVID, from Inverness, a student at King's College, Aberdeen, in 1669. [KCA]; eldest son of the deceased Robert Polson a merchant in Inverness, was admitted as a burgess and guild-brother of Inverness on 20 September 1686. [IMB.344]

POLSON, JOHN, a bailie of Inverness, references in 1642; a baillie and stent [tax] collector in Inverness on 30 August 1647; was appointed Dean of Guild in Inverness on 10 October 1648. [IMB.178/181/199]

POLSON, JOHN, from Inverness, a student at King's College, Aberdeen, in 1665. [KCA]

POLSON, ROBERT, from Inverness, a student at King's College, Aberdeen, in 1669. [KCA]

PONT, ZACHARY, son of Robert Pont the minister of St Cuthbert's in Edinburgh, graduated MA from Edinburgh University in 1583, printer to King James VI in 1590, minister at Bower from 1608 until 1618. Husband of Margaret Knox, parents of Samuel. [F.VII.113]

POPE, HECTOR, from Ross-shire, a student at King's College, Aberdeen, in 1667. [KCA]

POPE, HUGH, from Ross-shire, a student at King's College, Aberdeen, in 1665. [KCA]

POTENGER, MAGNUS, master of the <u>Katherine of Thurso</u> arrived in Aberdeen on 5 October 1664. [ASW.58]

POULL, ROBERT, mustered the militia in Inverness Chapel Yard on May 1684. [IBM.322]

PRUNTOCH, AGNES, wife of John Clyne in Wick, testament, 7 Augus 1661, Comm. Caithness. [NRS]

PURDIE, WILLIAM, a messenger, testament, Comm. Caithness, 1623. [NRS.CC4.8.1]

RAMSAY, ALEXANDER, a skipper in Inverness, a deed in 1677. [NRS.RD2.43.642]

RAMSAY, CHARLES, master of the <u>Amity of Inverness</u>, arrived in Inverness on 20 August 1691 from London. [NRS.E72.11.18]

RANKINE, PATRICK, a Lieutenant aboard the <u>Unity of Inverness</u>, a deed in 1668. [NRS.RD4.22.453]

REID, EPHRAIM, born around 1632 in Tain, son of Isaac Reid and his wife Elizabeth Hamilton, graduated from King's College, Aberdeen in 1654, a schoolmaster in Tain, Easter Ross, from 1655 until 1659, then at the Scots College in Rome in 1661, was ordained in 1663 at Ratisbon, settled in Erfurt, he returned to Scotland in 1685 as a missionary, he died around 1713. [TGSI.XLIV.96]

REID, WILLIAM, from Ross-shire, a student at King's College, Aberdeen, in 1650. [KCA]

REOCH, MARGARET, spouse of Donald Finlason in Skenand, testament, June 1663, Comm. Caithness. [NRS]

RITCHIE, CHARLES, from Inverness, a student at King's College, Aberdeen, in 1667. [KCA]

RICHIE, JAMES, was authorised to grant licenses to Highlanders and to residents of Inverness permitting them to sell whisky within Inverness-shire, on 25 May 1663. [IMB.215]

ROALD, MAGNUS, in Milton of Lyth, testament, February 1662, Comm. Caithness. [NRS]

ROBERTSON, A., a councillor of Inverness in 1642. [IMB.181]

ROBERTSON, ALEXANDER, and Mary Robertson, children of the deceased John Robertson a merchant in Poland and a burgess of Inverness, testament 21 October 1678 Comm. Inverness. [NRS]

ROBERTSON, COLIN, from Inverness, a student at King's College, Aberdeen, in 1665. [KCA]

ROBERTSON, GILBERT, of Kindeis, on 29 November 1647, was accused of deserting the town of Inverness 'in the time of the troubles'. [IMB.195]

ROBERTSON, GILBERT, was to participate in the trial of witches in Inverness on 28 April 1662. [IMB.213[

ROBERTSON, GILBERT, from Ross-shire, a student at King's College, Aberdeen, in 1677. [KCA]

ROBERTSON, HUGH, a stent [tax] collector in Inverness on 19 April 1672. [IMB.252]; treasurer of the burgh of Inverness in 1676. [TGSI.4.172]; treasurer of Inverness, was ordered to check the defences in East Street, also the arms of every man there on 29 March 1679. [IMB.279]; a baillie on 15 March 1680. [IMB.283]; took the Test Oath on 19 December 1681. [IMB.299]

ROBERTSON, JAMES, clerk of Inverness in 1642. [IMB.181]

ROBERTSON, JAMES, from Inverness, a student at King's College, Aberdeen, in 1665. [KCA]

ROBERTSON, JANET, relict of Donald Foullar, on 29 November 1647, was accused of deserting the town of Inverness 'in the time of the troubles'. [IMB.195]

ROBERTSON, JOHN, from Inverness, a student at King's College, Aberdeen, in 1673. [KCA]

ROBERTSON, LAURENCE, a burgess and baillie of Inverness, of the Inverness Burgh Court on 10 January 1603. [ICB.3]

ROBERTSON, WILLIAM, a burgess of Inverness, versus Donald Urquhart in Inverness in January 1603, for a debt due for a boll of victual and six firlots of malt which were supplied in August 1601. Also, versus Donald Urquhart for seven merks the value of two stone of lint supplied in February 1602. [ICB.4]

ROBERTSON, WILLIAM, Captain of the Inverness Militia on 25 May 1665. [IMB.216]

ROBERTSON, WILLIAM, a burgess of Inverness, testament 16 July 1666, Comm. Inverness. [NRS]

ROBERTSON, WILLIAM, a baillie of Inverness on 28 September 1670. [IMB.238]

ROBERTSON, Mr WILLIAM, of Inches, took the Test Oath on 19 December 1681. [IMB.299]; he, his family, and tenants, were granted the right of free passage over the bridge of Inverness because of the voluntary contribution msde towards ots erection, on 13 July 1683;
[IMB.317];
a juryman in an inquest in Inverness on 23 March 1686. [IMB.343]; was appointed as Commissioner for Inverness at the forthcoming Convention of Royal Burghs in Edinburgh on 5 July 1688. [IMB.7]

ROBERTSON, WILLIAM, from Ross-shire, a student at King's College, Aberdeen, in 1677. [KCA]

ROBISON, ANGUS, in Dornoch, Sutherland, paid his Hearth Tax in 1694. [NRS.E69.23.1.3]

ROBISON, WILLIAM, in Dornoch, Sutherland, paid his Hearth Tax in 1694. [NRS.E69.23.1.3]

ROBSON, MARJORIE, spouse of Alexander Harper, a mariner n Cromarty, and mother of Thomas Harper a shoemaker there, sasines from 1682.
[NRS.RS38.V.209]

RORIE BUY, [RUAIRIDH], JANET, an alleged witch in Inverness in 1662. [TGSI.IX.119]

RORISON, ALEXANDER, from Caithness, a student at King's College, Aberdeen, in 1675. [KCA]

ROSE, ALEXANDER, a baillie of Inverness on 28 September 1670. [IMB.238]; was appointed Provost of Inverness for 1676-1677, on 26 September 1676. [IMB.270]; was ordered to check the defences in Castle Street, also the arms of every man there on 29 March 1679. [IMB.279]; a baillie on 15 March 1680.
[IMB.283]

ROSE, Mr ALEXANDER, son of David Rose of Earlfunlie, was appointed schoolmaster of Inverness on 6 October 1673.
[IMB.256]

ROSE, ALEXANDER, baillie of Inverness, took the Test Oath on 19 December 1681. [IMB.299]

ROSE, CHRISTIAN, spouse of John Grant if Corriemonie, Urquhart, , testament 16 June 1632, Comm. Inverness. [NRS]

ROSE, DAVID, in Inverness, took the Test Oath on 19 December 1681. [IMB.299]

ROSE, GEORGE, from Ross-shire, a student at King's College, Aberdeen, in 1660. [KCA]

ROSS, GEORGE, born 1677, son of Alexander Ross of Pitkery, and his wife Joan Monro, of the Diocese of Ross, a student at the Scots College in Rome in 1698.
[RSC.124]

ROSE, HUGH, of Clava, acquired four acres of land on the Carse of Inverness on 25 April 1674. [IMB.260]

ROSE, JAMES, of Merkinch, Provost of Inverness in 1642. [IMB.181]

ROSE, JAMES, miller at the King's Mill and at Deirbocht Mill, was fined and imprisoned for using faulty measures on 30 October 1671. [IMB.249]

ROSE, JOHN, of Holme, Croy, testament 25 January 1632 Comm. Inverness. [NRS]

ROSE, JOHN, from Ross-shire, a student at King's College, Aberdeen, in 1658-1660. [KCA]

ROSE, JOHN, from Ross-shire, a student at King's College, Aberdeen, in 1675. [KCA]

ROSE, R., a councillor of Inverness in 1642. [IMB.181]

ROSE, ROBERT, was to participate in the trial of witches in Inverness on 28 April 1662. [IMB.213]

ROSE, ROBERT, a councillor of Inverness on 15 March 1680. [IMB.283]; took the Test Oath on 19 December 1681. [IMB.299]

ROSE, ROBERT, the younger, took the Test Oath on 19 December 1681. IMB.299]; a juryman in an inquest in Inverness on 23 March 1686. [IMB.343]; was appointed as Captain of a Militia Company to protect Inverness from McDonald of Keppoch and his rebels, 3 September 1688. [IMB.7]

ROSE, Mr WALTER, baillie of Inverness in 1642. [IMB.181]

ROSE, WALTER, from Ross-shire, a student at King's College, Aberdeen, in 1671. [KCA]

ROSE, WILLIAM, the elder, a burgess of Inverness, testament 6 June 1681 Comm. Inverness. [NRS]

ROSE, WILLIAM, of Merkinch, took the Test Oath on 19 December 1681. [IMB.299]; erected a barnyard on the town's common in error but was allowed to retain it for a year on 16 October 1682.[IMB.312]

ROSS, ALESTER, was captured at the Battle of Dunbar on 2 September 1650, was transported via London aboard the John and Sarah bound for New England on 8 December 1650, landed in Boston by 28 February 1651. [NWI.I.151]

ROSS, ALEXANDER, of Wester Grunyards, disposed of lands in Nigg to Alexander Hossack the minister at Kilmuir, Inverness-shire, on 20 January 1634. [NRS.GD1.125.3]

ROSS, ALEXANDER, from Ross-shire, a student at King's College, Aberdeen, in 1658.-1665. [KCA]

ROSS, ALEXANDER, junior, from Ross-shire, a student at King's College, Aberdeen, in 1658-1660. [KCA]

ROSS, ALEXANDER, a messenger, applied to be keeper of the Inverness Tolbooth on 27 June 1670. [IMB.242]

ROSS, ALEXANDER, of Nether Pitkerrie, son of Thomas Ross, minister at Fearn from 1670, dead by 1700, husband of Janet Munro. [F.VII.56]

ROSS, ALEXANDER, son of David Ross of Earlsmill, schoolmaster of Inverness, in 1673. [Inverness and Dingwall Presbytery Records.42]

ROSS, ALEXANDER, in Belinabelly of Drakes, Inverness-shire, was subjected to a precept of poinding for payment of a bond due to James MacIntosh a merchant in Inverness, on 31 July 1690. [NRS.GD23.10.302]

ROSS, ALEXANDER, a bailie of Inverness, on 9 April 1679. [NRS.AC7.5]; a deed in 1697. [NRS.RD4.81.7]

ROSS, ALEXANDER, in Dornoch, paid his Hearth Tax in 1694. [NRS.E69.23.1.3]

ROSS, AMBROSE, from Ross-shire, a student at the Monastery of Ratisbon, Germany, in 1708, died in 1714. [SIG.293]

ROSS, ANDREW, from Ross-shire, a student at King's College, Aberdeen, in 1667. [KCA]; minister at Contin in 1664, later at Urquhart from 1685 until his death in November 1712, husband of Anna Cumming. [F.7.47]

ROSS, ANDREW, a mason in Inverness, repaired the Town House in June 1675, also, in April 1677. [IMB.262/272]; a burgess of Inverness in 1682. [SHS.24.114]

ROSS, BARBARA, spouse of Donald Ross in Hiltoun, sister and heir of the deceased Thomas Ross of Preisthill, in Ross-shire in 1652, reference. [RGSS.X.11]

ROSS, BENJAMIN, from Ross-shire, a student at King's College, Aberdeen, in 1677. [KCA]

ROSS, CHRISTIAN, relict of William Dallas a merchant in Inverness, and spouse of Thomas Neilson a merchant there, a deed in 1697. [NRS.RD4.80.1367]

ROSS, DANIEL, probably from Ross-shire, a militiaman in Barbados in 1689. [H2.152]

ROSS, DAVID, son of Alexander Ross of Invercarron, [Inbhir Charran], Ross-shire, an officer of Mackay's Regiment in Danish Service in 1626, in Swedish Service in 1629. [TGSI.VIII.189][SAA.II.132]

ROSS, DAVID, brother of William Ross the younger, a bailie of Tain, was apprenticed to John Nicoll the younger, a merchant in Edinburgh on 10 September 1656. [REA]

ROSS, DAVID, from Ross-shire, a student at King's College, Aberdeen, in 1665. [KCA]

ROSS, DAVID, from Inverness, a student at King's College, Aberdeen, in 1673. [KCA]

ROSS, DAVID, in Dornoch, Sutherland, paid his Hearth Tax in 1694. [NRS.E69.23.1.3]

ROSS, DAVID, of Balnagowan, [Baile nan Gobhainn], Ross-shire, was admitted as a burgess and guilds-brother of Edinburgh on 4 May 1694, [REB]; and in 1708. [NRS.AC9.306]

ROSS, DONALD, in Dornoch, Sutherland, paid his Hearth Tax in 1694. [NRS.E69.23.1.3]

ROSS, DONALD JAMES, born 1672 son of Thomas Ross and his wife Christine Dunbar in Soyal, Ross-shire, he was educated at the Scots College in Rome from 1697 until 1699, was at Ratisbon Abbey in 1708, was ordained in 1714, died in November 1714. [TGSI.XLIV.100]

ROSS, FINLAY, in Ipswich, New England, in 1662. [LLNV.254]

ROSS, FINDLAY, a shipmaster in Inverness in 1681. [RPCS.XI.530]

ROSS, FINLAY, a burgess of Dornoch, a sasine ca.1671. [NRS.RS38.IV.135]

ROSS, GEORGE, son of Daniel Ross a litster, [dyer], in Tain, was, apprenticed to Thomas Wilson a litster in Edinburgh in 16.. [REA]

ROSS, GEORGE, in Newhaven, Connecticut, and Elizabeth, New Jersey, around 1658. [LLNV.254]

ROSS, GEORGE, from Ross-shire, a student at King's College, Aberdeen, in 1658-1659- 1660. [KCA]

ROSS, Captain GEORGE, of Lord Ross's troop of Dragoons, military papers from 1666 until 1713. [NRS.NRAS.276.2.22]

ROSS, GEORGE, a militiaman in Barbados in 1689. [H2.152]

ROSS, GEORGE, in Dornoch, Sutherland, paid his Hearth Tax in 1694. [NRS.E69.23.1.3]

ROSS, HELEN, sister and heir of the deceased Thomas Ross of Preisthill, in Ross-shire in 1652, reference. [RGSS.X.11]

ROSS, HUGH, from Ross-shire, a student at the Scots College in Rome in 1610. [RSC.103]

ROSS, HUGH, of Priesthill, a Lieutenant of Mackay's Regiment in Danish Service in 1626, in Swedish Service in 1629, was wounded at Oldenburg, Germany, in September 1627. [TGSI.VIII.187][SAA.II.125]

ROSS, HUGH, a soldier of Mackay's Regiment, was wounded at the Battle of Killiecrankie, Perthshire, on 27 July 1689. [RPCS.15.151]

ROSS, ISABEL, spouse of Alexander Cattenach in Delneis, sister and heir of the deceased Thomas Ross of Preisthill, in Ross-shire in 1652, reference. [RGSS.X.11]

ROSS, JAMES, Provost of Inverness, reference on 24 March 1641. [IMB.178]

ROSS, Lieutenant JAMES, was buried in St Elizabeth's, Danzig, [Gdansk], in 1643. [CRD]

ROSS, JAMES, of Merkinch, a councillor of Inverness on 20 April 1644. [IMB.182]; was appointed as Commissioner to the Convention of Burghs to be held in Kirkcaldy on 1 July 1644. [IMB.184]

ROSS, JAMES, was captured at the Siege of Worcester on 2 September 1651, then transported via London aboard the John and Sarah to Boston, New England, in December 1651, landed there in February 1652. [Suffolk Deeds.1.5/6]

ROSS, JAMES, born 1672, son of Thomos Ross and his wife Christina Dunbar in the Diocese of Ross, a student at the Scots College in Rome in 1697. [RSC.123]

ROSS, Mr JOHN, failed to appear before the High Burgh Court of Inverness on 10 January 1603. [ICB.3]

ROSS, JOHN, son of the Provost of Inverness, was admitted as a burgess of Aberdeen on 24 February 1624. [ABR]

ROSS, Mr JOHN, of Little Terrell. and his spouse Christina Monro, disposed of land in Nigg and in Tarbat, to James Innes of Inverbrecky, on 2 January 1610. [NRS.GD1.187.8]

ROSS, JOHN, was captured at the Battle of Dunbar on 3 September 1650, then transported via London aboard the Unity to Boston, New

England, in November 1651, settled in Kittery, Berwick, Maine, in 1656. [CEB]

ROSS, JOHN, was captured at the Siege of Worcester on 2 September 1651, then transported via London aboard the John and Sarah to Boston, New England, in December 1651, landed there in February 1652. [Suffolk Deeds.1.5/6]

ROSS, JOHN, from Ross-shire or Inverness, a student at King's College, Aberdeen, in 1659. [KCA]

ROSS, JOHN, a soldier of Captain Woodward's Company of Militia on Barbados in 1679. [H.2.156]

ROSS, JOHN, the burgh officer arrested David Baillie for operating a stall in Inverness though not being a freeman, on 10 January 1681. Baillie struggled with the burgh officers consequently he was put in the jugs at the market cross with a notice of his crime then was fined twenty pounds Scots. [IMB.288]; was appointed toll-keeper of the Inverness Bridge on 13 August 1683. [IBM.318]

ROSS, JOHN, in Catboll, a deed in 1697. [NRS.RD4.81.943]

ROSS, KATHERINE, spouse of William Innes in Dingwall, sister and heir of the deceased Thomas Ross of Preisthill, in Ross-shire in 1652, reference. [RGSS.X.11]

ROSS, LACHLAN, from Ross-shire, a student at King's College, Aberdeen, in 1667. [KCA]

ROSS, LACHLAN, son of William Ross a bailie of Tain, a sasine in 1670. [NRS.RS38.IV.20]

ROSS, MALCOLM, a merchant in Inverness, a deed in 1697. [NRS.RD4.80.12]

ROSS, MARGARET, the elder, sister and heir of the deceased Thomas Ross of Preisthill, in Ross-shire in 1652, reference. [RGSS.X.11]

ROSS, NICHOLAS, probably from Ross-shire, a Captain of Mackay's Regiment in Danish Service in 1626, in Swedish Service in 1629. [TGSI.VIII.187]

ROSS, ROBERT, a councillor of Inverness on 20 April 1644. [IMB.182]

ROSS, ROBERT, MA, minister at Lairg in 1658, then at Easter Logie, MA, minister at Urquhart from 1657 until 1665. [F.7.46/92]

ROSS, THOMAS, from Ross-shire, a student at King's College, Aberdeen, in 1587. [KCA]

ROSS, WALTER, a burgess of Tain, was admitted as a burgess and guilds-brother of Aberdeen on 2 September 1629. [ABR]

ROSS, Mr WALTER, a burgess of Inverness, was appointed as a Commissioner to negotiate with the government in Edinburgh, on 24 June 1646; a stent [tax] a baillie and collector in Inverness on 30 August 1647. [IMB.190/193]

ROSS, WALTER, a mason in Fortrose, a sasine ca.1670. [NRS.RS38.153]

ROSS, WALTER, from Ross-shire, a student at King's College, Aberdeen, in 1677. [KCA]

ROSS, WILLIAM, of Shandwick, born 1593, son of Robert Ross of Kinloch minister at Alness, graduated MA from King's College, Aberdeen, in 1614, minister at Fearn from 1644 until 1660, died at Shandwick on 20 April 1663, married [1] Elizabeth Campbell, [2] Isobel Douglas. [F.VII.56]

ROSS, WILLIAM, graduated MA from St Andrews University in 1653, minister at Edderton from 1665 until his death in April 1679, husband of Isabel McCulloch. [F.VII.53]

ROSS, WILLIAM, in Ardneill, brother and heir of the deceased Thom Ross of Preisthill, in Ross-shire in 1652, a reference. [RGSS.X.11]

ROSS, WILLIAM, of Sandwick, was granted the lands of Ulladell and others in Ross-shire, which had been apprised from Margaret Ross the elder, Isobel, Helen, Katherine, and Barbara Ross sisters of the deceased Thomas Ross of Priesthill, and from Alexander Catanach in Delneis, spouse to said Isobel, William Innes in Dingwall spouse to said Katherine, and Donald Ross in Hiltoun spouse to the said Barbara, also from Hugh Ross in Easter Fearn, and William Ross in Ardneill, on 12 August 1652. [RGSS.X.17]

ROSS, WILLIAM, minister at Edderton, [Eardarden], Ross-shire, a sasine ca.1667. [NRS.RS38.III.284]

ROSS, WILLIAM, from Ross-shire, a student at King's College, Aberdeen, in 1667-1677. [KCA]

ROSS, WILLIAM, a drummer, applied to be keeper of the Inverness Tolbooth on 27 June 1670. [IMB.242]

ROSS, WILLIAM, probably from Ross-shire, a militiaman in Barbados in 1689. [H2.152]

ROY, ANDREW, in Dornoch, Sutherland, paid his Hearth Tax in 1694. [NRS.E69.23.1.3]

ROY, IVER, in Corriarinstill, Kingussie, testament 14 November 1631 Comm. Inverness. [NRS]

ROY, KATHERINE, spouse of Thomas Kemp a tailor, a sasine dated around 1682. [NRS.RS38.V.367]

RUTHVEN, PATRICK, a merchant burgess of Dundee, was granted property in the Chanonry of Ross, on 22 December 1654. [RGSS.X.356]

SADGE, THOMAS, a burgess of Inverness, testament 14 May 1667 Comm. Inverness. [NRS]

SANDERSON, WILLIAM, a baillie of Dornoch in 1603. [OPS.II.644]

SCARLET, MARION, wife of John Cogill in Wattin, testament, June 1664, Comm. Caithness. [NRS]

SCOTT, DAVID, was authorised to grant licenses to Highlanders and to residents of Inverness permitting them to sell whisky within Inverness-shire, on 25 May 1663. [IMB.215]

SCOTT, DAVID, a Sergeant of the Inverness Militia on 25 May 1665. [IMB.216]

SCHAW, Mr ADAM, applied to become schoolmaster at Inverness Grammar School in February 1685. [IMB.330]

SHAW, ANDREW, a merchant in Inverness, a sasine in 1665. [NRS.RS38.III.278]; a stent [tax] collector in Inverness on 19 April

1672. [IMB.252]; a councillor on 15 March 1680. [IMB.283]; took the Test Oath on 19 December 1681. [IMB.299]

SHAW, AGNES, spouse of Donald Fraser a smith in Inshes, testament 17 July 1667 Comm. Inverness. [NRS]

SHAW, ANGUS, a sasine around 1673. [NRS.RS38.IV.300]

SHAW, ANGUS, and a child, in Ballenicreig, Barra, Outer Hebrides, in 1703. [NRS.CH1.2.512]

SHAW, DONALD, in Delnavert, testament 16 August 1632 Comm. Inverness. [NRS]

SHAW, DONALD, with three children, in Barra, Outer Hebrides, in 1703. [NRS.CH1.2.5.1]

SCHEVES, ALEXANDER, of Muirton, successfully bid for land at the Chaplaincy of the Green in Inverness on 13 June 1681. [IMB.293]

SCHIEVES, THOMAS, a councillor of Inverness on 20 April 1644. [IMB.182]

SHILTHOMAS, JAMES, son and heir of the late James Shilthomas in various lands in the parish of Halkirk, Caithness, on 17 September 1672. [NRS.GD139.405]

SHIRES, THOMAS, of Muirtoun, the younger, was granted Easter Moniack, [Mon Itheig], Inverness-shire, which formerly pertained to Thomas Fraser of Strechen, on 2 August 1653. [RGSS.X.169]

SIM, MARY, spouse of William McAndrew in Conveth, testament 3 September 1677 Comm. Inverness. [NRS]

SIMONSON, HEW FRASER, in Boleskin, Inverness, a sasine around 1679. [NRS.RS38]

SIMPSON, ALEXANDER, in Kilterne, as bailie to Hugh Monro, a sasine, witnessed by Lauchlan McKenzie, the apparent of Assynt, Hector McKenzie his brother, Andrew Monro son of John Monro the portioner of Clunes, and Alexander McCady a student in Alness, registered in the Inverness Sasines on 29 September 1692. [SRS. Munro of Foulis Writs]

SIMPSON, DONALD, a burgess of Fortrose, husband of Agnes McLey, a sasine around 1675. [NRS.RS38.IV.461]

SINCLAIR, ABRAHAM, in James City County, Virginia, in 1656. [EVI]

SINCLAIR, ADAM, probably from Caithness, in St Lucy's, Barbados, in 1678. [H2.45]

SINCLAIR, ALEXANDER, from Caithness, a student at King's College, Aberdeen, in 1677. [KCA]

SINCLAIR, ALEXANDER, of Dunbeath, a student at King's College, Aberdeen, in 1677. [KCA]

SINCLAIR, ALEXANDER, with 1 acre, 1 servant, and 7 slaves in St Michael's, Barbados in 1679. [H2.458]

SINCLAIR, DAVID, a mariner aboard HMS Hampton Court, probate 1697 Prerogative Court of Canterbury. [TNA]

SINCLAIR, JOHN, of Staimster, a deed dated 1695. [NRS.RD4.76.660]

SINCLAIR, ALEXANDER, of Sixpennyland, participated in the saving and salvage of the Pelsor of Amsterdam in the Pentland Firth in 1706. [NRS.AC9.239]

SINCLAIR, ANDREW, born 1614 probably in Caithness, to Sweden as a musketeer in Colonel Robert Stuart's Regiment in 1635, Regimental commander by 1678, enobled in Sweden in 1680, died in 1689. [SHR.IX.276]

SINCLAIR, CHARLES, from Caithness, a student at King's College, Aberdeen, in 1661. [KCA]

SINCLAIR, DAVID, probably from Caithness, a Cavalry officer in Sweden in 1651, was killed at the Battle of Warsaw in 1656. [SHR.IX.275]

SINCLAIR, DUNCAN, a rebel who was transported via Leith to Jamaica in August 1685. [RPCS.XI.136]

SINCLAIR, EDMOND, in Westmoreland County, Virginia, in 1656. [EVI]

SINCLAIR, EDWARD, in Barbados, however probate 25 November 1682 in Jamaica.

SINCLAIR, FRANCIS, son of Sir James Sinclair of Murkle, Major of Mackay's Regiment in Danish Service in 1626, in Swedish Service in 1629, was enobled in Sweden in 1645. [TGSI.VIII.186] [SHR.IX.275][SAA.II.132]

SINCLAIR, FRANCIS, in Latherone, Caithness, a bond dated 3 August 1674. [NRS.RD3.37.22]

SINCLAIR, FRANCIS, of Stircock, disposed of the lands of Sibster and others to his son George Sinclair in 1675. [NRS.NRAS.3094.462]

SINCLAIR, GEORGE, son of Mr John Sinclair of Olbuster, was apprenticed to John Ker a merchant in Edinburgh on 24 November 1630. [REA]

SINCLAIR, GEORGE, of Scrabster, was apprenticed to William Dick of Braid a merchant in Edinburgh on 1 August 1638. [REA]

SINCLAIR, GEORGE, Earl of Caithness, and Lady Mary Campbell, daughter of the Marquis of Argyll, an ante-nuptial marriage contract, dated July 1657. [NRS.GD112.25.131]

SINCLAIR, GEORGE, a merchant in Wick, Caithness, a bond dated 20 April 1674. [NRS.RD4.35.103]

SINCLAIR, GEORGE, a shoemaker in Wick, a bond dated 20 April 1674. [NRS.RD4.35.104]

SINCLAIR, GEORGE, from Ulbster, Caithness, a student at King's College, Aberdeen, in 1675. [KCA]

SINCLAIR, GEORGE, from Stircock, Caithness, a student at King's College, Aberdeen, in 1675. [KCA]

SINCLAIR, HELEN, wife of Captain Kenneth Urquhart, sasines in 1695. [NRS.RS38.VI.19/59]

SINCLAIR, HUGH, of Brugh, a deed in 1697. [NRS.RD3.87.555]

SINCLAIR, Sir JAMES, was granted the Sheriffdom of Caithness, by King Charles II on 30 July 1651. [NRS.GD1.212.56]

SINCLAIR, Sir JAMES, of Murkill, a soldier in Danish service from 1626 [SAA.II.134]; testament, 22 October 1662, Comm. Caithness. [NRS]

SINCLAIR, JAMES, of Lybster, a bond dated 6 February 1674. [NRS.RD3.35.237]

SINCLAIR, JAMES, a seaman from Scourie, Sutherland, indented for five years' service at Hudson Bay on 16 March 1683. [HBRS.9.86]

SINCLAIR, Sir JAMES, of Canesby, a deed in 1697. [NRS.RD4.81.43]

SINCLAIR, JAMES, of Stempster, in 1704. [NRS.AC9.82]

SINCLAIR, JEAN, in Surry County, Virginia, in 1655. [EVI]

SINCLAIR, JEAN, spouse of Magnus Corbat a shoemaker in Cromarty, a sasine ca.1685. [NRS.RS38.392]

SINCLAIR, Sir JOHN, of Greinland, a testament, 1622, Comm. Caithness. [NRS.CC4.8.1]

SINCLAIR, JOHN, of Geneis, was granted various lands in the neighbourhood of Wick, Caithness, on 22 May 1624. [NRS.GD96.477]

SINCLAIR, JOHN, of Obisdell, an officer in Danish Service from 1626. [NRS.GD84.161][SAA.II.125]

SINCLAIR, JOHN, third son of George Sinclair the 5th Earl of Caithness, Lieutenant Colonel of Mackay's Regiment in Swedish Service, was killed at Newmarke in the Upper Palatinate of Germany in 1632. [TGSI.VIII.185][SHR.IX.51] [SAA.II.127]

SINCLAIR, JOHN, in Domesdale Street, Inverness, a debtor for the stent in 1647. [IMB.194]

SINCLAIR, JOHN, in Surry County, Virginia, in 1655. [EVI]

SINCLAIR, JOHN, of Breynes, and his spouse Anna Mackay, in Ribisgill, purchased lands in the barony of Kintail, Sutherland, on 14 February 1657. [NRS.GD84.1.20.1]

SINCLAIR, JOHN, from Caithness, a student at King's College, Aberdeen, in 1658-1659-1660. [KCA]

SINCLAIR, JOHN, a mariner in Thurso, Caithness, husband of Margaret Rorieson, a sasine in 1660. [NRS.RS36.2.65]

SINCLAIR, JOHN, son of John Sinclair of Lybster, was apprenticed to John Neilson a merchant in Edinburgh on 17 July 1661. [REA]

SINCLAIR, JOHN, of Ulbster, Caithness, the younger, a bond dated 10 August 1674. [NRS.RD3.37.62]

SINCLAIR, JOHN, from Caithness, a student at King's College, Aberdeen, in 1677. [KCA]

SINCLAIR, JOHN, of Brabster, a deed dated 1695. [NRS.RD4.76.660]

SINCLAIR, JOHN, of Dunbeath, a deed in 1697. [NRS.RD4.81.128]

SINCLAIR, JOHN, in Perygreen, Old Albemarle County, North Carolina, before 1698. [NCSA.CR2.001]

SINCLAIR, JOHN, in Exeter, New Hampshire, died in 1699, probate 14 September 1700, New Hampshire.

SINCLAIR, MARGARET, in Charles City County, Virginia, in 1638. [EVI]

SINCLAIR, MARGARET, wife of John Nicoll a shipmaster in Thurso, testament, 17 February 1663, Comm. Caithness. [NRS]

SINCLAIR, MORRIS, in Charles City County, Virginia, in 1638. [EVI]

SINCLAIR, NEAL, in Charles City County, Virginia, in 1638. [EVI]

SINCLAIR, PATRICK, of Ulbster, a marriage contract with Elizabeth McKay, daughter of John McKay of Dilmet, dated 20 February 1640. [NRS.GD84.2.130]

SINCLAIR, PATRICK, probably from Caithness, probate 12 December 1674, Barbados.

SINCLAIR, PATRICK, from Stircock, Caithness, a student at King's College, Aberdeen, in 1675. [KCA]

SINCLAIR, PATRICK, a Notary Public and Messenger in Wick, [Inbhir Uige], Caithness, re an assignation by Elizabeth Sinclair, relict of William Sinclair of Dunbeath, [Dun Beithe], to their third son William Sinclair in 1694. [NRS.GD96.477]

SINCLAIR, PATRICK, of South Dun, a deed in 1697. [NRS.RD4.81.444]

SINCLAIR, RICHARD, Sergeant of Captain Scott's Company of Militia in Barbados in1679. [H2.87]

SINCLAIR, ROBERT, son of the laird of Mey, a student at King's College, Aberdeen, in 1657. [KCA] [NRS.RD3.36.364]

SINCLAIR, ROBERT, probably from Caithness, probate 14 February 1667, in Barbados. [RB.6.15]

SINCLAIR, ROBERT, was indentured in the Court of Quarter Sessions, Chester County, Pennsylvania, on 5 August 1697. [SG.29.1.13]

SINCLAIR, ROBERT, born 1685, a missionary of the Society for the Propagation of the Gospels at Newcastle, Delaware from 1709 to 1711. [SCHR.14.147]

SINCLAIR, SOLOMON, probably from Caithness, was captured at the Siege of Worcester in 1651, was transported via London aboard the John and Sarah to New England in November 1651. [Suffolk Deeds, 1-56] [NWI.I.153]

SINCLAIR, WILLIAM, servant to John, Earl of Sutherland, was admitted as a burgess of Aberdeen on 22 April 1624. [ABR]

SINCLAIR, Sir WILLIAM, of May, was granted various lands around Dingwall, Easter Ross, on 28 February 1654, which formerly pertained to Rorie McKenzie of Tollie. [RGSS.X.266]

SINCLAIR, WILLIAM, from Caithness, a student at King's College, Aberdeen, in 1663-1671. [KCA]

SINCLAIR, WILLIAM, possibly from Caithness, married Margery Butler, in Christchurch, Barbados, on 23 September 1661. [PR]

SINCLAIR, WILLIAM, quit rent in Delaware in 1671. [NYHist.MS.Dutch.28]

SINCLAIR, WILLIAM, in Latheron, and Jean Gordon, a minute of a marriage contract dated 3 July 1674. [NRS.RD

SINCLAIR, WILLIAM, from Caithness, a student at King's College, Aberdeen, in 1677. [KCA]

SINCLAIR, WILLIAM, of May, a deed in 1697. [NRS.RD4.81.107]

SINCLAIR, WILLIAM, a mariner aboard the Resolution who died in the East Indies, probate 1690 Prerogative Court of Canterbury. [TNA]

SINCLAIR, WILLIAM, born 1686 in Scotland, was indentured in the Court of Quarter Sessions, Chester County, Pennsylvania, on 14 July 1697. [SG.29.1.13]

SINCLAIR, WILLIAM, was admitted to the Scots Charitable Society in Boston in 1699. [NEHGS/SCS]

SINCLAIR, WILLIAM, in Hoy, Caithness, brother of Patrick Sinclair of Ulbster, a bond in 1702. [NRS.SC14.78.17.3]; and a tack [lease] to Donald Campbell of Middletoun of Halkirk, Caithness, in 1706. [NRS.SC14.78.17.4]

SINCLAIR, ..., of the Owners Adventure, died in Virginia, probate July 1697, Prerogative Court of Canterbury. [TNA]

SKINNER, FINDLAY, a debtor for the stent in Kirk Street, Inverness, in 1647. [IMB.194]

SKINNER, JOHN, a fisherman in Cromarty, a sasine ca. 1681. [NRS.RS38.V.128]

SMITH, ALEXANDER, in Inglishtoun, [A'Ghall-Bhaile], Inverness-shire, testament 15 November 1630, Comm. Inverness. [NRS]

SMYTH, CHRISTIAN, wife of William Sinclair a merchant Thurso, the elder, testament, 7 February 1662, Comm. Caithness. [NRS]

SMITH, GEORGE, a carpenter in Inverness, testament 20 November 1679, Comm. Inverness. [NRS]

SMITH, JAMES, from Ross-shire a student at King's College, Aberdeen, in 1661. [KCA]

SMITH, JAMES, master mason, who built a stone bridge at Inverness, was granted the freedom of Inverness on 10 May 1680. [IMB.284]

SMYTH, WILLIAM, graduated MA from St Andrews University in 1645, minister at Bower, [Bagair], Caithness, from 1640, died in Thurso in 1669. Husband of Sara Davidson, parents of Elizabeth Smyth. [F.VII.114]

SNODDIE, ANDREW, in Papigo, testament, 7 August 1661, Comm. Caithness. [NRS]

SPEEDIMAN, ALEXANDER, a merchant baillie of Fortrose, husband of Elspeth Dunbar, a sasine in 1661. [NRS.RS38.1.1]

SQUARE, ALEXANDER, a juryman in an inquest in Inverness on 23 March 1686.[IMB.343]

STEPHEN, WILLIAM, eldest son of William Stephen the elder a burgess of Inverness, was admitted as a burgess and guilds-brother there on 8 November 1686. [IMB.7]

STEVEN, WILLIAM, was appointed as Lieutenant of a Militia Company, to protect Inverness from McDonald of Keppoch and his rebels, on 3 September 1688. [IMB.7]

STUART, AGNES, spouse of John Murray a burgess of Inverness, testament 20 June 1667, Comm. Inverness. [NRS]

STUART, WILLIAM, from Inverness, a student at King's College, Aberdeen, in 1663. [KCA]

STEWART, ALEXANDER, master of the Amity of Inverness trading between Rotterdam, Holland, and I399ness from 1682 until 1685. [NRS.E72.11.4/5/6/7/8/9/10]; a shipmaster burgess, a sasine in 1701. [NRS.RS29.IV.95]

STEWART, Mr JAMES, schoolmaster of Inverness on 3 December 1663. [IMB.217]; resigned on 20 September 1669 then to become a minister. [IMB.237]

STEWART, JAMES, treasurer of Inverness on 28 September 1670. [IMB.238]; a stent [tax] collector in Inverness on 19 April 1672. [IMB.252]; burgh treasurer on 15 March 1680. [IMB.283]; a baillie, took the Test Oath on 19 December 1681. [IMB.299]

STEWART, JAMES, eldest son of baillie James Stewart of Inverness, was admitted as a burgess and guild-brother of Inverness on 20 September 1686. [IMB.344]

STEWART, JOHN, a baillie of Inverness on 25 September 1654. [IMB.209]; testament 8 May 1669 Comm. Inverness. [NRS]

STEWART, KATHERINE, at the Overmill of Abernethy, testament 1 August 1676, Comm. Inverness. [NRS

STEWART, WILLIAM, a mariner from Inverness died upon the Redbridge, probate 1698, Prerogative Court of Canterbury. [TNA]

STRONACH, JOHN, a gunsmith, portioner of Little Allan, formerly at Fearn, [Na Fearnan], husband of Margaret McCulloch, parents of Andrew Stronach, a sasine ca.1673. [NRS.RS38.IV.392]

SUPER, BESSIE, spouse of John Barbour a merchant in Inverness, testament 6 July 1680, Comm. Inverness. [NRS]

SUTHERLAND, ADAM, from Caithness, a student at King's College, Aberdeen, in 1658. [KCA]

SUTHERLAND, ALEXANDER, in York County, Virginia, in 1654. [EVI]

SUTHERLAND, ALEXANDER, from Sutherland, a student at King's College, Aberdeen, in 1671. [KCA]

SUTHERLAND, ALEXANDER, from Inverness, a student at King's College, Aberdeen, in 1677. [KCA]

SUTHERLAND, Mr ALEXANDER, was appointed schoolmaster of Inverness Grammar School in March 1685. [IMB.330]; master of Inverness Grammar School from 1685 to 1686, received 170 merks in payment of annual salary. [IMB.7]

SUTHERLAND, ANDREW, a Notary Public and Depute Sheriff Clerk of Inverness, a sasine dated 9 October 1664. [NRS.GD23.3.14]

SUTHERLAND, ANGUS, from Sutherland, a student at King's College, Aberdeen, in 1669. [KCA]

SUTHERLAND, ANSELL, [?], was captured at the Siege of Worcester in 2 September 1651, then transported via London aboard the John and Sarah bound for New England in December 1651, landed in Boston in February 1652. [Suffolk Deeds, 1/5-6] [NWI.I.153]

SUTHERLAND, ARTHUR, a student at King's College, Aberdeen, in 1670. [KCA]; graduated MA from King's College, Aberdeen, in 1674, minister at Edderton from 1680 until his death in April 1708, husband of Janet Ross. [F.VII.53]

SUTHERLAND. DAVID, from Sutherland, a student at King's College, Aberdeen, in 1661. [KCA]

SUTHERLAND, GEORGE, of Forss, Caithness, husband of Jean Gray, a sasine in 1661. [NRS.RS38.I.20]

SUTHERLAND, GEORGE, of Forss, Caithness, a student at King's College, Aberdeen, in 1678. [KCA]

SUTHERLAND, GILBERT, in James City County, Virginia, in 1655. [EVI]

SUTHERLAND, HUGH, from Caithness, a student at King's College, Aberdeen, in 1657. [KCA]

SUTHERLAND, ISAAC, a militiaman in Barbados in 1679. [H2/132]

SUTHERLAND, JAMES, son of William Sutherland in Dornoch, was apprenticed to David Wilkie a merchant in Edinburgh on 16 October 1644. [REA]

SUTHERLAND, Mr JAMES, minister of Inverness, to assist the town council in dealing with witches, on 14 April 1662. [IMB.211]; was to participate in the trial of witches on 28 April 1662. [IMB.213]

SUTHERLAND, JAMES, in Dornoch, Sutherland, paid his Hearth Tax in 1694. [NRS.E69.23.1.3]

SUTHERLAND, JAMES, of Langwell, and Anna Sinclair, a marriage contract, referring to Reisgill, Latheron, Caithness, dated December 1699. [NRS.CS228.S.1.44]

SUTHERLAND, JAMES, a mariner aboard HMS Hampshire probate 1692 Prerogative Court of Canterbury. [TNA]

SUTHERLAND, JANET, spouse of Andrew McKillican a cordiner burgess of Inverness, testament 26 August 1669 Comm. Inverness. [NRS]

SUTHERLAND, JOHN, Earl of Sutherland, also Lord Strathnavar, was admitted as a burgess and guilds-brother of Aberdeen, on 22 April 1624. [ABR]

SUTHERLAND, JOHN, of Clyne, the younger, a student at King's College, Aberdeen, in 1661. [KCA]

SUTHERLAND, JOHN, from Caithness, a student at King's College, Aberdeen, in 1671-1676. [KCA]

SUTHERLAND, JOHN, in Dornoch, Sutherland, paid his Hearth Tax in 1694. [NRS.E69.23.1.3]

SUTHERLAND, KENNETH, Lord Sutherland, a Jacobite in 1715, fought at Sheriffmuir, escaped to Sweden, returned but was imprisoned in the Tower of London, moved to Russia in 1722, an Admiral of the Russian Navy, died on 30 March 1734. [SP.II.212][NRS.GD2.4.308-310]

SUTHERLAND, MARGARET, in Dornoch, Sutherland, paid her Hearth Tax in 1694. [NRS.E69.23.1.3]

SUTHERLAND, OLIVER, in Dornoch, Sutherland, paid his Hearth Tax in 1694. [NRS.E69.23.1.3]

SUTHERLAND, PATRICK, was captured at the Siege of Worcester on 2 September 1651, then transported via London aboard the John and Sarah bound for New England in December 1651, landed in Boston in February 1652. [Suffolk Deeds, 1/5-6][NWI.I.153]

SUTHERLAND, RICHARD, a Corporal of Thomas McKenzie's Company in Denmark in 1628. [SAA.II.124]

SUTHERLAND, ROGER, a militiaman in Lieutenant Colonel Thomas Lewis's Company in Barbados on 6 January 1679. [H2.101]

SUTHERLAND, THOMAS, a militiaman of Colonel Colleton's Company in Barbados on 9 March 1679. [H2.119]

SUTHERLAND, WALTER, from Sutherland, a student at King's College, Aberdeen, in 1676. [KCA]

SUTHERLAND, WILLIAM, a drummer of Mackay's Regiment in Denmark in 1628. [SAA.II.120]

SUTHERLAND, WILLIAM, in Rumster, a bond dated 23 September 1661. [NRS.RD4.3.314]

SUTHERLAND, WILLIAM, from Sutherland, a student at King's College, Aberdeen, in 1668-1674. [KCA]

SUTHERLAND, ..., a Lieutenant of Mackay's Regiment in Danish Service in 1626, in Swedish Service in 1629, was promoted in Ruthven's Regiment. [TGSI.VIII.188]

SWANSON, CHRISTIAN, spouse of John Taylor, in Clairden, testament, June 1664, Comm. Caithness. [NRS]

TAIT, WILLIAM, in Kirk, testament, 27 June 1661, Comm. Caithness. [NRS]

TARRES, JOHN, servant to Lord Lovat, was admitted as a burgess and guilds-brother of Aberdeen on 31 August 1634. [ABR]

TARRES, PATRICK, in Mullochard, testament 25 March 1678, Comm. Inverness. [NRS]

TAYLOR, ALEXANDER, in Inverness in 1643. [IMB.193]

TAYLOR, ALEXANDER, grieve of Lovat, testament 25 March 1668, Comm. Inverness. [NRS]

TAYLOR, ARTHUR, a merchant in Thurso, husband of Margaret Munro, a sasine ca.1699. [NRS.RS38.VI.384]

TAYLOR, DONALD, from Inverness, a student at King's College, Aberdeen, in 1673. [KCA]

TAYLOR, JAMES, son and heir of the deceased Donald Taylor in Inverness, whose lands were apprised from him on 14 December 1654. [RGSS.X.356]

TAYLER, JAMES, a seaman, third son of the late John Tayler a merchant in Inverness, was admitted as a burgess and guildsbrother there on 11 October 1686. [IMB.7]

TAYLOR, KATHERINE, spouse of William Fraser, the elder, a shoemaker burgess of Inverness, testament 8 September 1680, Comm. Inverness. [NRS]

TAYLOR, MARJORIE, spouse to Robert Poull a burgess of Inverness, testament 17 September 1668, Comm. Inverness. [NRS]

THOMSON, DAVID, a smith in Tain, offered to settle in Inverness to take charge of the burgh clock for three years, a salary, and the freedom and liberty of Inverness, on 2 September 1682. [IMB.308]

THOMSON, JAMES, was appointed as Lieutenant of a Militia Company, to protect Inverness from McDonald of Keppoch and his rebels, 3 September 1688. [IMB.7]

THOMSON, JAMES, a merchant in Inverness in 1708. [NRS.AC9.302]

THOMSON, JOHN, son of Alexander Thomson a burgess of Chanonry of Ross, a sasine ca.1663. [NRS.RS38.II.91]

THOMSON, WILLIAM, a stent [tax] collector in Inverness on 19 April 1672. [IMB.252]; was appointed as Captain of a Militia Company, to protect Inverness from McDonald of Keppoch and his rebels, 3 September 1688. [IMB.7]

TOLME, WILLIAM, a merchant baillie of Fortrose, formerly in Forres, [Farrais], Moray, husband of Margaret Speidiman, sasines from around 1681. [NRS.RS38.V.691]

TOSH, JANET, in Rogart, spouse of Thomas Dickson a burgess of Dornoch, a sasine in 1666. [NRS.RS38.III.106]

TRENT, Captain JAMES, a merchant, late in Inverness, now in Pennsylvania aboard HMS Charles probate 1698, PCC. [TNA]

TRENT, MAURICE, a merchant in Leith, settled a debt of two hundred and twenty pounds Scots due to Inverness by his deceased brother William Trent, on 21 March 1681. [IMB.289]

TRENT, WILLIAM, was admitted as a burgess and guilds-brother of Aberdeen on 6 May 1634. [ABR]; a merchant in Inverness, testament 9 May 1677, Comm. Inverness. [NRS]

TRENT, WILLIAM, born in Inverness around 1655, a merchant in Inverness, built a pier and bulwark at Inverness dock, and was granted five years lease of the anchorage and shore dues on 24 May 1675, [IMB.261]; emigrated to Pennsylvania in 1682, later in New Jersey, settled on the Delaware River 32 miles from Philadelphia, moved to Philadelphia, Pennsylvania in 1703, an Assemblyman and Judge, founder of Trenton, N.J., was admitted to the Scots Charitable Society of Boston in 1697, died in 1714. [SCS] [NJSA.II.88/89]

TROUP, WILLIAM, a messenger, applied to be keeper of the Inverness Tolbooth on 27 June 1670. [IMB.242]

TUACH, GEORGE, in Easter Kessock, [Ceasag], and his wife Katherine McCulloch, son of John Tuach of Logiereich, a sasine ca.1709. [NRS.RS38.VIII.14]

TULLOCH, JANET, spouse of Donald Forbes a miller in Cantray, Croy, testament 18 October 1634, Comm. Inverness. [NRS]

TULLOCH, LUDOVIC, a servant of the Earl of Seaforth, was admitted as burgess and guilds-brother of Aberdeen on 4 March 1675. [ABR]; husband of Christine Dallas, brother of Alexander Tulloch of Tanachie, a sasine around 1683. [NRS.RS38.V.200]

URCHARD, THOMAS, from Ross-shire, a student at King's College, Aberdeen, in 1663. [KCA]

URQUHART, ALEXANDER, of Dunlugus, [Dunlugas], was granted the lands and barony of Cromarty on 6 August 1658. [RGSS.X.665]

URQUHART, ALEXANDER, a shipmaster in Cromarty, a bond dated 13 July 1674. [NRS.RD2.37.647]

URQUHART, ANDREW, a monk of the Monastery of St James in Wurzburg, Germany, before 1630. [SF.279]

URQUHART, ANDREW, a member of Fraser's Dragoons in 1646 during the Wars of the Three Kingdoms.

URQUHART, BENJAMIN, a sailor in Cromarty, son of Alexander Urquhart there, a deed in 1697. [NRS.RD4.80.34]; a sasine, ca. 1697 [NRS.RS38.VI.468]

URQUHART, DAVID, in Inverness on 25 October 1667. [IMB.233]; a jailor, was accused of opening the prison doors, was punished by sitting in the stocks, having his wages withdrawn, and be discharged on 24 October 1670. [IMB.245]

URQUHART, GEORGE, a mariner on HMS Expedition probate 1692 Prerogative Court of Canterbury. [TNA]

URQUHART, JAMES, in Inverness on 25 October 1667. [IMB.233]

URQUHART, JOHN, Governor of Birsen in 1655. [MGIF.Map 2]

URQUHART, JOHN, a merchant in Stornaway, [Steornablagh], Lewis, husband of Anna McKenzie, son of Henry Urquhart a carpenter in Cromarty, sasines from ca.1675 until ca.1719. [NRS.RS38.IV.415; VI.295; VII.265/475/493/496/515]

URQUHART, JOHN, son of Urquhart of Cromarty, was admitted as a burgess and guilds-brother of Aberdeen on 15 March 1635. [ABR]

URQUHART, Sir JOHN, of Cromarty, was admitted as a burgess and guilds-brother of Aberdeen on 6 April 1665, [ABR]; deeds in 1674/1697. [NRS.RD4.34.509; RD4.80.1126; RD4.81.167]

URQUHART, JOHN, a musician, died aboard HMS Princess Anne in Jamaica, probate 1697, Prerogative Court of Canterbury. [TNA]

URQUHART, JONATHAN, of Cromarty, deeds in 1685. [NRS.RD4.56.20; 57.145]

URQUHART, Sir THOMAS, born 1611 son of Thomas Urquhart of Cromarty and his wife Christian Elphinstone, was educated at King's College, Aberdeen, a Royalist soldier in the Rising at Inverness in 1648, possibly was Quartermaster of Fraser's Dragoons in 1646 during the Wars of the Three Kingdom, later fought at the Siege of Worcester under King Charles II, where he was captured and imprisoned in the Tower of London until released by Oliver Cromwell in 1652, he returned to Cromarty, he was a noted translator and writer, died in 1660.

URQUHART, THOMAS, son of Alexander Urquhart, minister at Cromarty from 1673 until deprived in 1678. [F.VII.4]

URQUHART, WILLIAM, a tailor in Inverness, testament 14 March 1669, Comm. Inverness. [NRS]

URQUHART, WILLIAM, from Cromarty, a student at King's College, Aberdeen, in 1674. [KCA]

URQUHART, WILLIAM, a minister who emigrated to America in 1702, settled on Long Island, New York, died in 1709. [EMA.61]

VOIR, ANDREW MCWILLIAM, failed to appear before the High Burgh Court of Inverness on 10 January 1603. [ICB.3]

WALLACE, Mr JAMES, brought money from Orkney for the bridge, on 22 May 1682. [IMB.304]

WARSSE, DONALD, in Seater, Caithness, was to be apprehended as a rebel in 1670. [RPCS.III.194]

WARSE, JAMES, in Seater, Caithness, was to be apprehended as a rebel in 1670. [RPCS.III.194]

WARSSE, SWANN, in Seater, Caithness, was to be apprehended as a rebel in 1670. [RPCS.III.194]

WATSON, ANDREW, a ship carpenter in Fortrose, Easter Ross a sasine ca.1693. [NRS.RS38.291]

WATSON, DAVID, from Inverness, a student at King's College, Aberdeen, in 1670. [KCA]

WATSON, DONALD, in Daltullich, testament 9 July 1680, Comm. Inverness. [NRS]

WATSON, GEORGE, a wobster, [weaver], in Inverness, testament 22 July 1630, Comm. Inverness. [NRS]

WATSON, JOHN, from Inverness, a student at King's College, Aberdeen, in 1676. [KCA]

WATSON, ROBERT, a glover in Fortrose, son of Andrew Watson a shoemaker there, a sasine ca.1709. [NRS.RS38.VII.513]

WAUS, GEORGE, in Inverness, was fined twenty pounds and withdrawal of burgess rights for fraud, on 28 June 1675. [IMB.263]; he was restored to his burgess rights on 1 May 1676. [IMB.267]

WAUSS, JAMES, failed to appear before the High Burgh Court in Inverness on 10 January 1603. [ICB.3]

WAUS, JOHN, of Loch Slin, Ross-shire, failed to appear before the High Burgh Court of Inverness on 10 January 1603. [ICB.3]

WAUS, ROBERT, failed to appear before the High Burgh Court of Inverness on 10 January 1603. [ICB.3]

WAUS, THOMAS, a councillor of Inverness in 1642. [IMB.181]

WEMYSS, ALEXANDER, a fisherman in Inverness, a deed in 1672. [NRS.RD3.28.817]

WEMYSS, BEATRIX, relict of Sir James Fraser of Brey, and mother of James Fraser, sasines dating from 1666 to 1695. [NRS.RS38.III.177/187; IV.181; V.164]

WILLIAMSON, DAVID, and wife Marion Andrew, a testament, June 1663, Comm. Caithness. [NRS]

WILLIAMSON, JAMES, a shoemaker in Inverness on 24 January 1687. [IMB.7]

WILLIAMSON, JOHN, a burgess of Thurso, Caithness, in 1649, between 1653 and 1656 he made several raids into Caithness. [BW.146]

WILLOX, GEORGE, a merchant in Cromarty, was admitted as a burgess and guilds-brother of Aberdeen on 23 September 1673. [ABR]

WILSON, ROBERT, a juryman in an inquest in Inverness on 23 March 1686. [IMB.343]

WORRACH, DONALD, in Skinene, testament, 8 August 1664, Comm. Caithness. [NRS]

WRIGHT, ALEXANDER, the elder, in Englishtoun, Wardlaw, testament 26 February 1678, Comm. Inverness. [NRS]

WRIGHT, alias MCINTYRE, DONALD, husband of Christian Hood, in Inverchannich, a sasine, between 1679 and 1694. [NRS.RS38.V.308]

WYLLIE, DONALD, in Scrabster, Caithness, a testament, 8 August 1664, Comm. Caithness. [NRS]

WYLLIE, HENDRIE, a fisherman in Thurso, Caithness, a testament in 1663, Comm. Caithness. [NRS]

YEAMAN, PATRICK, a wobster, [weaver], in Borlum, testament 5 March 1670, Comm. Inverness. [NRS]

YOUNG, DONALD, in Inverness on 25 October 1667. [IMB.233]

YOUNG, HELEN, spouse of Donald Clerk a baker in Fortrose, ESTER Ross, a sasine, 1679. [NRS.RS38.V.18]

YOUNG, JEAN, spouse of Thomas Williamson a Writer to the Signet, a sasine around 1696. [NRS.RS38.VI.342]

YOUNG, JOHN, a tailor in Inverness on 25 October 1667. [IMB.233]

YOUNG, ..., master of the Caithness Fisher petitioned for protection against capture by privateers, in 1710. [NRS.AC10.97]

YOUNGER, ROBERT, in Thurso, Caithness, testament, in June 1664, Comm. Caithness. [NRS]

www.ingramcontent.com/pod-product-compliance
Lightning Source LLC
Chambersburg PA
CBHW070945230426
43666CB00011B/2565